Dressing for
the Lord

David W. Cloud

Dressing for the Lord
Copyright 2007 by David W. Cloud
This edition May 2017
ISBN 978-1-58318-106-5

Published by Way of Life Literature
P.O. Box 610368, Port Huron, MI 48061
866-295-4143 (toll free) • fbns@wayoflife.org
http://www.wayoflife.org

Canada: Bethel Baptist Church,
4212 Campbell St. N., London, Ont. N6P 1A6
519-652-2619

Printed in Canada by
Bethel Baptist Print Ministry

Contents

Dedication

I dedicate this book to the wife of my youth. We were married in August 1976, and not on even one occasion has she failed to demonstrate that modest femininity that comes only from a Christ-centered heart. She is a true Proverbs 31 woman. "Who can find a virtuous woman? for her price is far above rubies. ... Favour is deceitful, and beauty is vain: but a woman that feareth the LORD, she shall be praised" (Proverbs 31:10, 30).

Introduction

There was a time, just a few years ago, when a message like the one contained in this book was heard from fundamentalist and independent Baptist pulpits across the world, but that is no longer the case. All too often, any kind of preaching about clothing has become an oddity, an embarrassment, or a type of "legalism." The resistance of the rock & roll culture to such preaching is so pervasive that many pastors have decided to ignore the matter of dress, thus the battle is lost simply because the ground is abandoned.

Yet if ever there ever were a time when preachers need to warn their people about clothing issues, it is today. Modern society is drenched with indecency. A Vogue fashion show would make ancient Corinth blush. Standards of morality are not to be left to the pew. Surely it is the obligation of the preacher to set forth these things. Has God not spoken on this issue? We know that holiness is a matter of the heart, but is it not a matter of the body, as well? What man has ever lusted after a woman's heart? How, then, can we ignore these parts of Scripture and refuse to preach them boldly and uncompromisingly? That is what the New Evangelical does. There are some things he will not preach, and separation is one of them. But the Bible speaks as much about moral separation as it does about ecclesiastical separation. The faithful Bible-believing preacher cannot ignore either.

Those who are crying "legalism" today are hypocritical in this matter. They decry the old-time preacher for the lines he draws, but they, too, draw lines for clothing. Will they allow a woman to teach a Sunday School class in a bikini or a man to sing a special in lipstick, a dress, and high heels? No, and there are other types of attire they do not allow. They draw lines; they have standards. And if it is right to draw a line in clothing, it is wise to draw the line after the Bible's principles rather than the world's.

Let's make a clear difference between ourselves and the world. Let's not be afraid of being a "peculiar people, zealous of good works." Let's stand in the old paths. Those who are giving up high, plain standards of holiness in dress and moving closer and closer to the fashions of the world should remember that the world is moving farther and farther from God's Word.

A Church's Modesty Standard Must Go beyond Mere Written Rules

I want to make it as clear as possible that when I talk about "dressing for the Lord" I am not talking about merely putting a bunch of rules on Christian women. I believe specific dress standards are necessary in churches, but a church's standards must go beyond any specific written standard. The church must teach both men and women the why of modesty and the biblical principles thereof, and the church must find a way to reach the hearts of the females so that they are not merely obeying specific rules of dress but they love Jesus Christ so much that they want to measure everything in their lives by what pleases Him.

This is the approach we take in this book. To lay a solid Bible foundation for modesty, we are going to give a careful exegesis of about 25 key Bible passages from Genesis to 1 John. We are going to develop Bible principles that can be applied to any nation or culture. As foreign missionaries we are concerned about teaching Christian women that the Bible's principles for modesty can work anywhere. Furthermore, we strongly believe in dealing with the heart of this matter and not the mere externals.

Please don't judge me or this book by something you might have witnessed somewhere else.

I realize that in some independent Baptist circles "dress standards" are not much more than a part of a package of what is considered to be proper church life and perhaps a badge of honor to impress others, and in this context modesty often doesn't reach beyond a few written rules.

One man wrote to say: "I am not against strong Bible preaching, but I go into countless churches that have an immature, uneducated flock because no one ever takes the time to teach them the Word. It's much easier to preach on a topic than to actually study and prepare then teach the Scripture. I think we as Independent Fundamental Baptist are for the most part impatient."

This man has a point. Topical preaching is certainly not wrong; in fact, it is necessary; but preachers and teachers need to stand back and make sure that the church is a serious Bible-training institution that produces biblically-educated people who are truly prepared to serve Jesus Christ. And there is indeed a great need for preachers and teachers to be patient, looking for that spiritual fruit that can only come through the Holy Spirit. We cannot change the heart, but we can teach and pray and fast and yearn and wait on God.

The Woman Has an Obligation

Many women protest that the men should just watch their eyes, and we agree wholeheartedly that a Christian man is responsible to guard his eyes, but that is only one side of the coin. The woman also has a responsibility. Since the woman's figure is a powerful attraction to the man, the Christian woman is responsible to dress so that she does not draw his attention in a sensual manner.

There are far too many women in fundamental Baptist churches who are sensual and stubborn and who resist the teaching of Scripture and the preaching of God's men and the pleas of the tempted. This is probably the greatest reason why so many preachers simply ignore this issue in their preaching. There are just too many stubborn females in the congregation who cause trouble anytime someone mentions modest apparel. The preacher should be brave enough to buck them, but it is not an easy matter and many do not think it is worth the trouble.

If you are a female reading this book, I trust that I have not described you in the previous paragraph, because as long as you are stubborn and sensual there is no way that I or any other preacher can help you to be modest. We can show you what the Bible says about modesty and we can show you what men say about how that sensual dress affects them, but we cannot change your heart. The foundation of a modest Christian life is a heart surrendered to Christ.

The Importance of Reproof

The Bible teaches us that even after we are saved we still have the "flesh" and the "old man," which is the sin nature that we inherited from Adam.

> "For I know that in me (that is, in my flesh,) dwelleth no good thing: for to will is present with me; but how to perform that which is good I find not" (Romans 7:18).

> "This I say then, Walk in the Spirit, and ye shall not fulfil the lust of the flesh. For the flesh lusteth against the Spirit, and the Spirit against the flesh: and these are contrary the one to the other: so that ye cannot do the things that ye would" (Galatians 5:16-17).

> "If so be that ye have heard him, and have been taught by him, as the truth is in Jesus: That ye put off concerning the former conversation the old man, which is corrupt according to the deceitful lusts; and be renewed in the spirit of your mind; and that ye put on the new man, which after God is created in righteousness and true holiness" (Ephesians 4:21-24).

Since the believer has an indwelling propensity to sin, an enemy that lives within, he cannot trust his own understanding and his own heart. Note the following important exhortations:

> "Trust in the Lord with all thine heart; and LEAN NOT UNTO THINE OWN UNDERSTANDING. In all thy ways acknowledge him, and he shall direct thy paths" (Proverbs 3:5-6).

> "THE HEART IS DECEITFUL ABOVE ALL THINGS, and desperately wicked: who can know it?" (Jeremiah 17:9).

> "HE THAT TRUSTETH IN HIS OWN HEART IS A FOOL: but whoso walketh wisely, he shall be delivered" (Proverbs 28:26).

It is for this reason that the Bible instructs the believer to receive reproof and correction. This is one of the themes of the book of Proverbs, which is a book that teaches practical godly living. This book tells us that our attitude toward reproof is a measure of the condition of the heart.

"For the commandment is a lamp; and the law is light; and reproofs of instruction are the way of life" (Proverbs 6:23).

"He is in the way of life that keepeth instruction: but he that refuseth reproof erreth" (Proverbs 10:17).

"The way of a fool is right in his own eyes: but he that hearkeneth unto counsel is wise" (Proverbs 12:15).

"Only by pride cometh contention: but with the well advised is wisdom" (Proverbs 13:10).

"The ear that heareth the reproof of life abideth among the wise. He that refuseth instruction despiseth his own soul: but he that heareth reproof getteth understanding" (Proverbs 15:31-32).

When I am reproved by God's Word, what is my attitude? Do I think that I already know everything and don't need reproof? Do I have a proud attitude? Am I contentious?

I need to understand that godly, biblical reproof is for my own good. The Bible says, "For whom the Lord loveth he chasteneth, and scourgeth every son whom he receiveth" (Hebrews 12:6). God does not correct us because He hates us but because He loves us, and righteousness is always the best for us. "In the way of righteousness is life; and in the pathway thereof there is no death" Proverbs 12:28).

Having a right heart attitude toward biblical reproof is a major part of the battle in knowing God's will.

My prayer should be, "Lord, keep my heart right with Thee; help me be wise in receiving reproof; help me not be puffed up and foolish and carnal."

The Origin of Clothing

"And they were both naked, the man and his wife, and were not ashamed" (Genesis 2:25).

"And when the woman saw that the tree was good for food, and that it was pleasant to the eyes, and a tree to be desired to make one wise, she took of the fruit thereof, and did eat, and gave also unto her husband with her; and he did eat. And the eyes of them both were opened, and they knew that they were naked; and they sewed fig leaves together, and made themselves aprons" (Genesis 3:6-7).

"Unto Adam also and to his wife did the LORD God make coats of skins, and clothed them" (Genesis 3:21).

Nakedness only became a problem because of man's fall. Before this the man and woman were naked and there was nothing wrong with their nakedness. The problem came when man sinned and his heart became darkened and he began to think sinful thoughts. His heart became "deceitful above all things, and desperately wicked" (Jer. 17:9). It began to spew forth "evil thoughts, murders, adulteries, fornications, thefts, false witness, blasphemies" (Mat. 15:19). Prior to this, man's thoughts were only pure and holy and right.

Both the nudist and the fashion designer say, "We have bodies; why not enjoy them?" but they are willfully ignorant of the Fall and its grave consequences.

Since the Fall, nakedness must be covered properly according to God's standards. When Adam and Eve became aware of their nakedness they instinctively tried to cover it themselves, but their covering was not right before God. The fig leaf aprons were not acceptable. It left their chests and thighs and legs exposed. From then until now the issue of modesty is not something that God has left to men to decide.

There is a heavenly standard for earthly modesty, and that is what we are going to examine in this book.

As a starting point, we can learn a lot just by considering what a modest covering was according to God's standard at the very beginning of man's history.

The main lesson here is that the clothing covered the individual's nakedness. The Bible says God made them "coats," but that does not refer to a mere jacket. The Hebrew word translated "coats" in Genesis 3:21 is translated "robe" in Isaiah 22:21 and in 2 Samuel 13:18 it describes Tamar's robe of many colors. As opposed to Adam and Eve's aprons, God provided robes that covered them. This teaches us that clothing should cover the chest entirely and properly. In Proverbs 5:19 the Bible says to the married man, "… let her breasts satisfy thee at all times." That is restricted to the marriage bed. Other than this, the woman needs to take special care to cover herself properly and not draw attention to this part of her body. The robes doubtless also covered their legs and thighs. In Isaiah 47:2-3, where God pronounces judgment upon Babylon, we find that the uncovering of the leg and thigh is nakedness by God's standard. "Take the millstones, and grind meal: uncover thy locks, make bare the leg, uncover the thigh, pass over the rivers. Thy nakedness shall be uncovered, yea, thy shame shall be seen: I will take vengeance, and I will not meet thee as a man."

We will see that there are other principles of modesty in Scripture, but proper covering of one's nakedness is a starting point and that is what we see at the very dawn of man's history.

Clothing Is a Language

It is important to understand that clothing is a language. It is a "social message," a fashion "statement."

Wikipedia defines fashion as "a prevailing mode of expression." It acknowledges that "every article of clothing carries a cultural and social meaning" and observes that "humans must know the code in order to recognize the message transmitted."

The knowledge of this is the engine that drives the fashion industry, and the child of God needs to understand it, as well.

I need to ask myself what message is my clothing broadcasting?

American fashion designer Rachel Zoe said, "Style is a way to say who you are without having to speak" (goodreads.com).

"Clothes change our view of the world, and the world's view of us" (Feminist writer Virginia Woolf, *Orlando*, chapter 4).

"Choose your clothes for your way of life" (American actress Joan Crawford, azquotes.com).

"Style is a simple way of saying complicated things" (Jean Cocteau, French designer, playwright, filmmaker, goodreads.com).

"Every day I'm thinking about change" (Miuccia Prada, Italian fashion designer, brainyquote.com)

"Basically I'm trying to make men more sensitive and women stronger" (Miuccia Prada, Italian fashion designer, brainyquote.com).

"What you wear is how you present yourself to the world, especially today, when human contacts are so quick. Fashion is instant language" (Miuccia Prada, Italian fashion designer, "Interview: 'Fashion Is How You Present Yourself,'" *Wall Street Journal*, Jan. 18, 2007).

"I've realized that fashion is a very powerful instrument that ... allows you to transmit ideas and shape opinion" (Miuccia Prada, Italian fashion designer, "Interview: 'Fashion Is How You Present Yourself,'" *Wall Street Journal*, Jan. 18, 2007).

"... there are sociological interests that matter to me, things that are theoretical, political, intellectual and also concerned with vanity and beauty that we all think about but that I try to mix up and translate into fashion" (Miuccia Prada, Italian fashion designer, brainyquote.com).

George Harrison of the Beatles, who rebelled against the way his father wanted him to act and dress, testified: *"Going in for flash clothes, or at least trying to be a bit different ... was part of the rebelling. I never cared for authority"* (Hunter Davies, *The Beatles*, p. 39).

Note that Harrison's flash clothing and non-conformity was intimately associated with his rebellion.

Mary Quant, the fashion designer generally credited with inventing the mini-skirt in the mid-1960s, admitted that her aim was to entice men and promote licentiousness. She wanted something "daring" and "controversial," which refers to pushing moral boundaries, something sexually immodest. It was regarded as a "symbol of liberation." Some European countries banned the mini-skirt, saying it was an invitation to rape (Mary Quant, interview with Alison Adburgham, *The Guardian*, October 10, 1967). Quant also promoted a short hair style for women. Her fashions were statements and her clothing was a language.

Vivienne Westwood, who helped create the rock punk look, said, "I think fashion is the strongest form of communication there is. ... It's only interesting to me if it's subversive: that's the only reason I'm in fashion, to destroy the word 'conformity'" (Jon Savage, *Time Travel: Pop, Media and Sexuality 1976-96*, p. 119).

David Kidd once posed the following question to a young college girl who was inquiring about his family's conservative dress: "If you are shopping and see a girl in a long, loose fitting dress, what is your first impression of her?" Without any hesitation, she answered "that she is probably religious." He concluded, "It behooves us to recognize that our manner of dress is a statement that either reflects or contradicts our Christian purpose" (*The Fall and Rise of Christian Standards*, p. 154).

Hair styles are also statements. Long hair on men and short hair on women are not merely harmless fashions, a mere sign of the times, but are statements of rebellion against God's created order (1 Corinthians 11:14-15).

The androgynous unisex image is not innocent. It was created by rock musicians who intended to overthrow tradition. One of the rock songs of the 1960s called upon young men to grow their hair long and "let your freak flag show." David Lee Roth of Van Halen testified: "[My long hair] is a flag. It's Tarzan. I'll always be anti-establishment" (cited by John Makujina, *Measuring the Music*, p. 73).

Dennis Wilson of the Beach Boys sported long hair and popularized the "surfer cut" in the early 1960s. Commenting on the significance of this hair length, Wilson's biographer observes: "The 'surfer cut,' as it came to be known, was a radical thing to behold in 1962. Few parents would permit their sons to sport the look" (Jon Stebbins, *Dennis Wilson: The Real Beach Boy*, p. 24). Dennis Wilson was a rebel and his appearance was merely a reflection of this. Observe, too, that the "surfer cut" was not that long compared to the long hair that came afterwards, but it was just long enough to be a bold statement of non-conformity. Small fashion changes can have large consequences.

Paul McCartney of the Beatles flippantly acknowledged their role in overthrowing sexual distinctions: "There they were in America, all getting house-trained for adulthood with

15

their indisputable principle of life: short hair equals men; long hair equals women. Well, we got rid of that small convention for them. And a few others, too" (Barbara Ehrenreich, "Beatlemania: Girls Just Wanted to Have Fun," cited by Lisa Lewis, *The Adoring Audience: Fan Culture and Popular Media*, p. 102).

Where did the "small convention" of "short hair equals men; long hair equals women" come from? Why was this an "indisputable principle of life" in America prior to the onslaught of Beatles' style rock & roll in the 1960s? The answer is that America, because of its vast number of churches, had been influenced by the Bible in these things. It was Bible principles that the Beatles ridiculed and sought to overthrow.

Abercrombie & Fitch, the clothing company that markets "edgy" clothing featuring loose sexuality, is "best known for its REBELLIOUS ATTITUDE" ("Flip-Flops, Torn Jeans, and Control," *Business Week*, May 30, 2005). Thus even the world recognizes the message of Abercrombie & Fitch clothing. They don't merely sell clothing; they sell an attitude via a certain style of clothing.

In "The World according to Abercrombie and Fitch," David Seel observed: "SUCCESSFUL BRANDS IN AMERICA DON'T SELL PRODUCTS. THEY SELL LIFESTYLES" (*Critique*, 2000).

The upscale unisex Pusch brand was developed by two brothers who realized as teenagers that "music had its own subculture, complete with a lifestyle and a style of dress" ("Groovin' to the Right Tune: A Lifestyle Brand of Clothes Inspired by Calgary's Music Scene Rocks the Competition," *Alberta Venture*, October 2007, p. 12). The Pusch brand is a reflection of the rock & roll dance scene.

Even the small details of clothing are significant as a language. Referring to the denim jean market in the 21st century, the web site fashionera.com observes that this market "is status ridden and has CODED TRIBAL SIGNS

16

AND SIGNALS with it's not so subtle stitching, logos, tabs, decorative pockets, shading and distressing."

Therefore, clothing styles are not innocent. Each style preaches a message. Fashion designers are change agents.

Pantsuits preach the feminist's message of equality of the sexes.

Tight fitting, low cut, short and skimpy styles preach the world's message of loose sexuality.

Ripped jeans preach the message of a cheap affectation of poverty, of "I don't care" and thus slovenliness, and of moral casualness.

Slit skirts preach the message of sexual flirtation.

God's people must beware of sending the wrong message with their clothing. We must understand that the clothing industry is not in submission to God and cares nothing about submitting to His Word.

It doesn't do to say, "Well, my tight, ripped jeans don't preach that message TO ME." The important point is not what message the clothing preaches to any particular individual who wears it, but what message it preaches in the context of its history and in the context of society at large and to those who are forced to look at it.

The child of God should ask, "Who invented this type of dress, this particular fashion, and what was his or her objective?"

> "Wherefore be ye not unwise, but understanding what the will of the Lord *is*" (Eph. 5:17).

> "Whether therefore ye eat, or drink, or whatsoever ye do, do all to the glory of God. Give none offence, neither to the Jews, nor to the Gentiles, nor to the church of God: Even as I please all men in all things, not seeking mine own profit, but the profit of many, that they may be saved" (1 Cor. 10:31-33).

The Captains of the Fashion Industry

What type of men and women control the fashion industry that produces the clothing styles desired by teenage girls and women? Who are the captains of this industry?

The first fact we should understand is that the fashion industry is shot through and through with homosexuality. Speaking at a panel discussion of Generation X Fashion in New York City in 2005, Tara Subkoff stated that fashion "is a gay man's profession" ("A Gay Day for Fashion," *New York Times*, Dec. 15, 2005). Melanie McDonagh, fashion reporter, said: "I asked a couple of fashionista friends of mine to name a single major heterosexual male designer, and they were stumped" ("Designers Parody Women at Paris Fashion Show," *Daily Mail*, July 20, 2004).

Consider the following admission from an encyclopedia of Gay, Lesbian, Bisexual, Transgender, and Queer Culture under the section on "Fashion":

> "Historians of the modern gay experience have documented the large proportion of gay men who have worked in creative fields (such as fashion and the theater) and service industries (such as restaurants and catering). Ross Higgins, in his study of gay men's involvement in fashion in Montreal, has shown that gay men were involved at all levels of the fashion industry there. The same is undoubtedly true throughout North America and Western Europe. THROUGHOUT THE TWENTIETH CENTURY MANY OF THE TOP COUTURE FASHION DESIGNERS WERE GAY, EVEN THOUGH SOCIAL PRESSURE CALLED FOR THEM TO KEEP THEIR SEXUALITY QUIET IF NOT SECRET. Indeed, many of the greatest names in twentieth-century fashion were gay or bisexual, including such figures as Christian Dior, Cristóbal Balenciaga, Yves Saint Laurent, Norman Hartnell, Halston, Rudi Gernreich (who was one of the founding members of the first American homophile

organization, the Mattachine society), Giorgio Armani, Calvin Klein, and Gianni Versace."

The following are a few examples of the moral debauchery and anti-Bible attitude that permeates this industry.

Christian Dior (1905-57)

Known as "the man who made the world look new," the Frenchman Christian Dior launched the "house of Dior" in 1947. His designs revolutionized women's dress. In his male fashions he went after the "manly and depraved look" ("Christian Dior: The Man Who Made the World Look New," fashionwindows.com). For the female his fashions emphasized the woman's figure, making her appear more curvaceous ("Christian Dior," Wikipedia). He did this by form clinging dresses and "bustier-style bodices, hip padding, wasp-waisted corsets and petticoats that made his dresses flare out from the waist." He named one suit the "Jean-Paul Sartre" in honor of the morally debauched philosopher. Dior was a homosexual. At age 14 a fortune teller predicted that women would make him famous. He religiously carried a string of lucky charms.

Calvin Klein (b. 1942)

Klein is a bi-sexual fashion designer who has brazenly promoted sexuality in clothing and helped popularize sexy styles down to the level of "tweens." Klein has promoted highly indecent public advertisements for sexy underwear, both for men and women. His super tight jeans sold 200,000 pairs in one week when they appeared in 1978. A biography of Klein on AskMen.com observes: "Klein has become notorious for the nudity, blatant sexuality, and use of underage, prepubescent models in his ads ... While he has been married, his days as a bachelor hanging out at the famed Studio 54 could be considered questionable, as can his sexuality."

Gianni Versace (1946-1997)

Versace was an influential homosexual Italian fashion designer who was "influenced by Andy Warhol and modern abstract art" (Wikipedia). "He liked to create sexy clothes for his women, skin-tight with low cuts and high slits on the skirts. Versace was among the first to revive the cat suit, to bring back the mini skirt, to show tights worn as trousers, to bring the bustier out at night and bead it. In 1982 his dresses made with fine metal mesh first appeared and were a hit. … Versace has been referred to as the rock-and-roll designer and clients include Phil Collins, Bruce Springsteen, George Michael, Eric Clapton, Elton John, and Michael Jackson." Versace was shot to death in front of his mansion in July 1997 by a homosexual man.

Yves Saint Laurent

Yves Saint Laurent (1936-2008) was one of the most influential fashion designers of the 20th century. It was said: "There is virtually nothing about the way we dress or the way we shop now that was not a result of his 44-year career" ("Yves Saint Laurent Changed How We Dress," *Los Angeles Times*, June 5, 2008). He was a homosexual, spent time in psychiatric institutions, and was addicted to drugs. His long-time homosexual partner, Pierre Berge, said that Saint Laurent "played a part" in the liberation of women. In fact, he helped to enslave them to fashion and tempt them into rejecting their God-given femininity. He invented the pantsuit in 1966, as part of the rebellious rock & roll culture. Linda Grant observes that the pantsuit "put women on an equal sartorial footing with men and "is what fashion gave to feminism" ("Feminism Was Built on the Trouser Suit," *The Guardian*, June 3, 2008).

John Galliano

Galliano, who was British Designer of the year in 1988 and knighted in 2001, is a homosexual.

Paul Smith

Smith is a British fashion designer renowned for his multicolored pinstripes. He is infamous for his "naked lady" designs hidden inside cuffs or wallets. He has a collection of masculine attire for women.

Vivienne Westwood

Westwood created the punk fashion. Her second marriage was to Malcolm McLaren, the manager for the vile punk rock band The Sex Pistols. In 1971 they opened the SEX/Seditionaries fashion store in London. The punk look featured such things as leather bondage gear, safety pins, chains, spiked dog collars, outrageous makeup and hair. Wikipedia observes that Westwood revolutionized fashion and "the impact is still felt today." Her fashions were so influential that they have been shown at the Victoria and Albert Museum in London and the National Gallery in Australia. She stated that the only reason she is in fashion is to be subversive and to destroy the word 'conformity'" (Jon Savage, *Time Travel: Pop, Media and Sexuality 1976-96*, p. 119).

Giorgio Armani

The Italian Armani's designs for women "are inspired by men's wear" (Giorgio Armani, Infomat.com). He is a homosexual.

Tommy Hilfiger

Hilfiger said, "I knew exactly what I wanted to do: I wanted to build a brand of clothing around my own attitude and my own lifestyle." It is described as clothing "for the people." Thus it is all about self, a fulfillment of the prophecy in 2 Timothy 3:1-2 -- "This know also, that in the last days perilous times shall come. For men shall be lovers of their own selves..." It is rock & roll clothing. Hilfiger sponsored the vile Rolling Stones' 1999 "No Security" tour.

Mike Jeffries

Jeffries is the head of Abercrombie & Fitch, an influential trend-setting clothing company worth $2.6 billion. When Jeffries came to the company his "big idea was to make the new A&F sizzle with sex." In the article "Flip-flops, Torn Jeans, and Control," he is described as follows:

> "Jeffries is a man with many obsessions: youth, fashion, himself, his lucky shoes. ... A bonfire burns daily amid the tin-roofed buildings, where dance music blares nonstop. ... No matter the weather, he trots around the place in flip-flops, torn jeans, or shorts. Most mornings he lifts weights barefoot in the company gym. At home, a photo of a toned naked male torso shot by Herb Ritts hangs over the fireplace in his bedroom. ... A former colleague, Neil Dinerman, [says]: 'He would like to be a guy with a young body in California.' ... Jeffries leaves his black Porsche -- doors unlocked, with the keys between the seats -- at the same odd angle at the edge of the parking lot. Everyone knows why: Jeffries is superstitious about success. That's why he always goes through revolving doors twice. Associates have learned not to pass him in stairwells; he returns the courtesy. Then there are Jeffries' lucky shoes, a worn pair of Italian loafers that a secretary keeps in her desk. 'I put them on every single morning when I look at the numbers,' he says" (*Business Week*, May 30, 2005).

These are only a very few examples of the weirdness and moral perversion that can found among the captains of the fashion industry.

It should also be understood that these men and women have an influence that extends throughout the industry. Though their personal dress creations can cost as much as $15,000 and are beyond the reach of the average person, their philosophy and designs trickle down to the lowest level of the industry, to the Sears, Penney's, Wal-Marts, Coles (Australia), Marks & Spencers and Hennes & Mauritzs (Europe), and Tescos (England) of the world.

"Of all the cultural wolves that prey upon Christian principles, none has been more merciless toward virtuous, modest womanhood than modern fashion. ... From short shirts to tight tops, high-rise hem lines to low-rise jeans, each new craze dares women to cast aside their inhibitions and reveal themselves in a new and bolder way. Tragically, many Christian women have sacrificed the precious virtues of modesty, decency, and discretion to the ruthless determination of the cultural wolf whose appetite for them is never satisfied" (David Kidd, *The Fall and Rise of Christian Standards*, pp. 87, 88).

Isn't This Basically the Man's Problem?

Many women seem to think that the issue of modesty is basically the man's problem and that if he would keep his eyes to himself that would be the end of the matter.

The answer to this is that both the man and the woman have a grave responsibility.

Christian men most definitely should keep their eyes in check and say, with Job, "I made a covenant with mine eyes; why then should I think upon a maid?" (Job 31:1), and with David, "I will set no wicked thing before mine eyes..." (Psalm 101:3).

This is not to say, though, that Christian women can dress as they please because they have no responsibility in the matter. *If she knows that men are seriously tempted in the matter of sexual lust and if she knows that certain types of dress can cause more problems for men than others, why would a godly girl or woman not want to do everything she can not to cause a potential for stumbling?*

David was a man after God's own heart, the sweet Psalmist of Israel, a man who had determined not to set any wicked thing before his eyes; yet look at what happened to him after seeing a woman innocently (apparently) bathing on her roof.

Most women don't properly understand how powerful the visual element is to the man in the realm of sex and sensuality.

One man wrote to say: "I do believe most women just do not know how men think. Period. I BELIEVE THAT THERE IS A WHOLE SEGMENT, GROUP, CLASS OF WOMEN, WHO, IF THEY REALLY UNDERSTOOD MEN, WOULD CHANGE THEIR DRESS CODE, BECAUSE THEY DO WANT TO PLEASE GOD. ... *They just need to understand it's not just a list of do's and don'ts set forth to force them in to 'frumpiness,' but a desire of godly men to gain their cooperation in helping them NOT lust, and to not be stumbling blocks, because they just want to please God.*"

Anther man wrote: "I am a 24-year-old, unmarried man. I am very glad that you are asking us men about this issue, because it has been my experience that women truly do not understand the things that can run through a man's head when he sees an immodestly-dressed woman. ... Some women have told me that it is a man's fault for having such a dirty mind or for letting it get to a point where lust becomes a problem, but the fact is that men seem specifically prone to these types of thoughts."

The book *For Women Only: What You Need to Know about the Inner Lives of Men* by Shaunti Feldhan describes the powerful visual aspect of man's sexuality. Note the following statements:

> "[A] woman who is dressed to show off a great body is an 'eye magnet' that is incredibly difficult to avoid, and even if a man forces himself not to look, he is acutely aware of her presence. ... [When a group of men were asked what their reaction would be if they were sitting alone in a train station and a woman with a great body walked in and stood in a nearby line,] a whopping 98 percent put their response in 'can't *not* be attracted' categories (only 2 percent were unaffected). Interestingly, the results were essentially the same for men who described themselves as happily married believers. ...

> "One faithful husband whom I highly trust confessed, 'If I see a woman with a great body walk into Home Depot and I close my eyes or turn away until she passes, for the next half hour I'm keenly aware that she's in there somewhere. I'm ashamed to say that, more than once, I've gone looking down the aisles, hoping to catch a glimpse.'

> "I'd love to think that this man was an aberration--except that all the men I shared his quote with said, 'That's exactly right!' ...

"In addition, the man's initial temptation is often not only unintentional, but automatic. If the stimulus is there (a great figure in a right outfit), so is the response. As one man put it, 'It doesn't even register that I thought *great body* until two seconds later!' A man cannot prevent those *initial* thoughts or images from intruding.

"Don't believe me? Let me illustrate.

"Don't read this.

"No really, don't read it. Just look at the letters.

"Impossible, isn't it? There is no way to just notice the letters without reading the word. That's what it's like for a guy. His brain reads 'good body' without his even realizing it.

"One man provided this analogy. 'If you are nearsighted, everything is fuzzy without glasses. With your glasses, everything is in sharp focus. If a babe walks into Starbucks, other women sort of see fuzzy--all they see is that a woman is there. But all the men in the room suddenly have their 'glasses' on--that woman is in sharp focus, and it's really hard not to stare at her.'

"This distinction actually debunks the assumption that all the trouble starts because 'men have roving eyes.' A better understanding is that there are roving, under-dressed women--and men can't not notice their existence. ... The choice is the critical distinction between temptation and sin. Once an image intrudes in a man's head, he can either linger on it and possibly even start a mental parade, or tear it down immediately and ['bringing into captivity every thought'] as the Bible puts it. ... So although few men can stop an involuntary image from popping up in their heads, and few men can stop themselves from wanting to look, they can (and do) exercise the discipline to stop themselves from actually doing so" (Shaunti Feldhahn, *For Women Only: What You Need to Know about the Inner Lives of Men*, pp. 111-113, 120-123).

A knowledge of the man's make up as a fallen creature and the powerful temptation that the immodestly dressed female can be to him should help the Christian woman understand how imperative it is for her to dress properly.

The section on "Survey of Men on the Subject of Women's Dress" describes exactly what attracts men and what a problem immodest clothing is for them.

Bible Guidelines for Clothing
By Bruce Lackey

Introductory note by Brother Cloud: The following is by the late Bruce Lackey (1930-1988). He was a great blessing in my life. As a young man he played honky-tonk piano in bars. After his conversion he became serious about God's will and was a zealous student of Scripture. He read his Greek New Testament every day and taught and preached from the King James Bible, being convinced that it was expertly translated from the correct Hebrew and Greek manuscripts and believing that it needed no correction. He was the Dean of the Bible School at Tennessee Temple when I was a student there in the 1970s and he was the best Bible teacher I have ever had the privilege of sitting under. He was also a conscientious soul-winner and a master of sacred music styles on the piano. He taught his students that it was not right to use a bar-room style of music in the service of a holy God. In August 1976 he performed our wedding in a ceremony at his church in Tennessee. In the 1980s he traveled as a Bible conference preacher, and he died in 1988 of complications with medicine he was taking for an illness.

The thing I want to talk to you about tonight is Christian clothing. What do we mean when we say "Christian clothing"? Is that some particular article? No, we can't hang a particular suit or a particular dress up here tonight and say this is Christian. Rather, there are five questions that you need to ask yourself to answer the question, "What kind of clothing should I wear?" There are five questions, and I am going to support these by God's Word.

I hope you will get these down, because you are going to face this all your life. Fashions are going to change and new things are going to be brought out all the time. There is no use in me making up a list of what is good and what is not, because that would change next year. So these five principles from God's Word will help you to decide every single item, whether it be right or wrong to wear, male or female, adult or child.

Is it worn by the opposite sex?

The first question is this: Is it worn by the opposite sex? Turn back to Deuteronomy 22:5 for our beginning. Here is our first principle. When I am trying to decide whether or not I should wear a certain thing, my first question is "Is that item worn by the opposite sex?" In other words, I as a man should not wear anything that a woman would wear. And a woman should not wear anything that a man would wear.

> "The woman shall not wear that which pertaineth unto a man, neither shall a man put on a woman's garment: for all that do so are abomination unto the Lord thy God."

I am well aware of the fact that people resent using this verse because it is in the Old Testament. And many times people say we can't use that verse unless we are going to use the whole chapter. For instance, we wouldn't want to use verse nine. A lot of people violate that verse by planting two or three different kinds of seeds in the same plot of ground. Similarly, we've all violated verse eleven about wearing garments with different kinds of cloth. Nearly everything we have on is made out of a weave of different things. So how can we take verse five and not take verse nine or verse eleven?

The answer is that any principle found in the Old Testament which is repeated in the New Testament is for us today.

Let me prove that to you. Keep your place at Deuteronomy and go over to 1 Corinthians 10. In 1 Corinthians 10 we have a book written by a grace preacher. Nobody can deny that the Apostle Paul was a grace preacher. He preached that we're not under the law but under grace, and he wrote about that time and time again. Without a doubt he is a New Testament preacher. But I want you to notice that in this entire chapter of 1 Corinthians 10 he constantly uses the Old Testament Scripture to prove something. Look at verses one and two: "Moreover, brethren, I would not that ye should be ignorant, how that all our fathers were under the cloud, and all passed through the sea; And were all baptized unto Moses in the cloud and in the sea." That was taken from Exodus 13 and 14, in which passage we read about the cloud, and about the Red Sea parting, and how they walked across on dry land, which was similar to being baptized. They were covered with the water, even though not a drop of it touched them. Paul is referring to the Old Testament. Look at verse three: "And did all eat the same spiritual meat." That refers to Exodus 16, when God gave the manna from Heaven. That was called spiritual food. Verse four: "And did all drink the same spiritual drink: for they drank of that spiritual Rock that followed them: and that Rock was Christ." That refers to Exodus 17, when Moses took his rod and struck the rock, and God gave gushing water out of that flinty rock.

Notice that he is referring to several Old Testament incidents. Verse five: "But with many of them God was not well pleased: for they were overthrown in the wilderness." That is referring to Numbers 13 and 14. They refused to go into the land of Israel and inherit it, and they said, "We can't take it," and so God overthrew them in the wilderness. Many of them died.

Now look at verse six. "Now these things were our examples, to the intent we should not lust after evil things, as they also lusted." You see. It's not wrong to use the Old Testament to teach New Testament Christians to do something right. Paul did it.

Let's keep on going. Verse seven: "Neither be ye idolaters, as were some of them; as it is written, The people sat down to eat and drink, and rose up to play." Here he refers to Exodus 22:6. The Apostle says, "Don't you be like that." Verse eight: "Neither let us commit fornication, as some of them

committed, and fell in one day three and twenty thousand."
That is talking about Numbers 25. Verse nine: "Neither let us
tempt Christ, as some of them also tempted, and were
destroyed of serpents." That is talking about Exodus 17. You
remember about the brazen serpent being raised in the
middle of the camp, and so on.

Look at verse ten: "Neither murmur ye, as some of them
also murmured, and were destroyed of the destroyer." That is
found in Exodus 15, 16 and 17, among many other places;
they murmured several times.

Now look at verse eleven: "Now all these things happened
unto them for ensamples: and they are written for our
admonition, upon whom the ends of the world are come."
Two times in these chapter, in verse six and in verse eleven,
he tells us without a doubt that those Old Testament writings
were for us today. It is a foolish and fictitious objection when
someone says that we can't use the Old Testament for us
today. Here he very clearly outlines verse after verse,
experience after experience in the Old Testament, to prove
something that Christians ought to do right now. And that's
not the end. In the rest of the chapter he does it again and
again.

We see the same thing in 1 Corinthians 9:9-10:

> "For it is written in the law of Moses, Thou shalt not
> muzzle the mouth of the ox that treadeth out the corn.
> Doth God take care for oxen? Or saith he it altogether for
> our sakes? For our sakes, no doubt, this is written: that he
> that ploweth should plow in hope; and that he that
> thresheth in hope should be partaker of his hope."

Here again Paul says that the things in the Law of Moses
contain lessons for Christian living. We don't use oxen today
in western culture, and we don't therefore have to be
concerned about feeding oxen, but the abiding principle from
this law is that the worker should be rewarded for his labor,
whether in the physical or the spiritual realms.

31

Thus the Old Testament is for us today when rightly applied, and our rule in applying the Old Testament to Christian living is that any Old Testament principle repeated in the New Testament is for us today. Now you won't ever find a New Testament verse that says observe the sabbath day. That is the reason we don't do it. You won't find any New Testament verse that says we are to kill an animal and have a blood sacrifice. That's the reason we don't do it. But anything commanded in the Old Testament and repeated in the New Testament is for us today.

Is the teaching of Deuteronomy 22:5 repeated in the New Testament? Let's look at 1 Corinthians 11, where Paul refers to the appearance of man and woman. Specifically he talks about hair, but very clearly in 1 Corinthians 11 the Apostle says that the man and the woman ought to be different in their appearance. Notice verses four and five: "Every man praying or prophesying, having his head covered, dishonoureth his head. But every woman that prayeth or prophesieth with her head uncovered dishonoureth her head: for that is even all one as if she were shaven."

You see what he is saying? There is to be a difference between man and woman when they pray or prophesy. There is to be a difference. That is the same principle we saw back in Deuteronomy 22:5 -- "The woman shall not wear that which pertaineth unto a man, neither shall a man put on a woman's garment..." It is the same idea.

Paul goes on to talk about the length of the hair. Notice verses fourteen and fifteen: "Doth not even nature itself teach you, that, if a man have long hair, it is a shame unto him? But if a woman have long hair, it is a glory to her: for her hair is given her for a covering." Once again he underscores the principle that the appearance of men and women is to be different. Consequently, we have the same principle in Deuteronomy 22:5 repeated right here in the New Testament.

Further, Deuteronomy 22 verses 9-11, though not repeated in the New Testament, teach the principle of separation which is taught in the New Testament. These verses teach that God hates mixture. Consider how they are worded:

> "Thou shalt not sow thy vineyard with divers seeds: lest the fruit of thy seed which thou hast sown, and the fruit of thy vineyard, be defiled. Thou shalt not plow with an ox and an ass together. Thou shalt not wear a garment of divers sorts, as of woollen and linen together."

The Jews were not allowed to mix seeds or different types of material or an ox with an ass. This is the principle of separation, and it is definitely repeated in the New Testament, though the New Testament focuses on its spiritual application. Consider the following Scriptures:

> "No man can serve two masters: for either he will hate the one, and love the other; or else he will hold to the one, and despise the other. Ye cannot serve God and mammon" (Matthew 6:24).

> "Be ye not unequally yoked together with unbelievers: for what fellowship hath righteousness with unrighteousness? and what communion hath light with darkness? And what concord hath Christ with Belial? or what part hath he that believeth with an infidel? And what agreement hath the temple of God with idols? for ye are the temple of the living God; as God hath said, I will dwell in them, and walk in them; and I will be their God, and they shall be my people. Wherefore come out from among them, and be ye separate, saith the Lord, and touch not the unclean thing; and I will receive you" (2 Corinthians 6:14-17).

> "Love not the world, neither the things that are in the world. If any man love the world, the love of the Father is not in him. For all that is in the world, the lust of the flesh, and the lust of the eyes, and the pride of life, is not of the Father, but is of the world" (1 John 2:15-16).

All of these New Testament Scriptures teach that it is wrong for the believer to mix righteousness with unrighteousness or the world and Christ. We are separate from the evil things of the world. It is the same basic principle stated in Deuteronomy 22:9-10, though the Mosaic Law used carnal things to illustrate the principle while the New Testament uses spiritual.

Let me share something with you that is very interesting. I have in my library a book called The *Treasury of Scripture Knowledge*. It is one of the most beneficial books I have ever owned. It is simply a book of parallel references, just like the center reference column you have in your Bible, but it is greatly expanded. This book was printed over one hundred years ago, back when they weren't having many of the problems we are having today with women wearing men's clothes, and *vise versa*. So you couldn't say they were prejudiced about this subject when they put the cross references in that volume. The *Treasury of Scripture Knowledge* at Deuteronomy 22:5 has a parallel reference of 1 Corinthians 11:3-14. That's interesting, isn't it? You know what that proves? It proves that men that study the Bible, not just in our day but years ago, have seen that 1 Corinthians 11 contains the same principle that is stated in Deuteronomy 22:5.

I don't hesitate to use Deuteronomy 22:5 to prove that women ought not to wear men's clothes, and men ought not to wear women's clothes, any more than I would hesitate to use Psalm 23 at a funeral. You see, the truths are repeated in the New Testament.

I was also interested in what I found in the Keil and Deiletch commentary regarding this matter. That commentary was first printed more than a hundred years ago. Charles Spurgeon refers to Keil and Deiletch. Yet Keil and Deiletch say that Deuteronomy 22:5 was written to maintain the sanctity of the distinction of the sexes which was established by the creation of man and woman. In other words, anybody who reads the Bible can see that all the way through in every age and every testament God has said that He wants men and women to look different. Consequently we ought not to wear clothing that applies to the opposite sex.

Of course, the main issue that we are facing here is the matter of pants on women. It matters not what you call them, whether blue jeans or slacks or pant suits. It is a main problem today. People like to argue about this. They say you can't condemn pants on a woman unless you are going to say that women can't wear belts, because men wear belts. Likewise you would have to say that women can't wear socks, or shirts, because men wear socks and shirts.

What do we say about this? Consider some simple things to keep in mind. First, we are talking about the obvious. We're not talking about some hidden thing, like a belt, that doesn't have anything to do with the sex of the person, that doesn't have anything to do with the body.

Second, what do you look like when you wear these clothes? What do you look like from a distance? You've had the same experience that I've had of being out in public and seeing somebody at a distance and not being really sure if that person is a male or a female. You can't tell by the clothes, because girls wear pants just like boys do. They wear T-shirts just like boys do. The boys often have their hair just as long as the girls [or the girls' just as short as the boys'], so you look at someone from a distance and you often cannot tell if the person is a male or a female. The only way you can tell is to look at those portions of the body that distinguish between male and female, and by the way, that is the Devil's reason behind all of it. That is what he wants you to look at. He doesn't want you to look at somebody's head; he wants you to look other places. That is one of the things that makes this so wrong, and we need to see that. We should not wear clothing which at a distance would make anybody wonder whether we are male or female. And we should not wear those types of clothing that focus attention on the wrong parts of our bodies.

The best place to start on this is when the child is born. If you start when the child is born, you won't ever have to make any changes. If you don't start then, you'll always be wondering when you should make this change. Just start right in the beginning. Cut the baby boy's hair like a boy's hair should be cut, and don't put feminine clothes on him. Put pants on him. And if it is a girl, don't put pants on her; put a dress on her.

You see, all these questions that people argue about can be settled just by plain old common sense. The principle is to let the appearance be different enough that folks won't have any doubt. That's the way to answer it all. You don't have to get everybody's O.K. on this piece of clothing, or that one, just draw the line and determine to wear something that no one will ever have a doubt about. It's going to look like man's clothing. It's going to look like women's clothing.

What about women working out in the field? What about women working in factories? What about women who have to climb ladders? Don't they need something modest? Yes, they do need something modest. I used to see women out in the field picking cotton and so on. I used to see them wear overalls, but I also saw some of them put dresses on over their overalls. That was a common thing when I was a boy. Now I know that some of them didn't wear dresses over their overalls. Some of them did other things that were wrong, too. You know, too, there are some other things to wear, such as culottes, which are just as modest and still look feminine. That's what you ought to wear. If you can't buy any, get a sewing machine and learn how to sew. It's worth the expense and trouble to make that adjustment if you are going to have convictions.

Do not wear clothing that the opposite sex wears. And if you are in doubt about it, just don't and you will be safe. Just make sure that what you wear identifies you as a male or as a female, and not in a way that a person would have to look at the tempting zones of the body to tell whether you are a male

36

or female. That is what the Devil wants you to do, and surely you don't want to cooperate with the Devil on this matter.

What does it make others think of me?

Here is the second question you need to ask yourself about Christian clothing: What does it make others think of me? Lest you say it doesn't matter what other people think, let me read a verse or two of Scripture, and then let me read you some illustrations from modern literature which say that it does matter. In Proverbs 7:10 the Scripture has a warning to a young man against immorality: "And, behold, there met him a woman with the attire of an harlot, and subtil of heart." God is warning about a woman dressed like a harlot. Now the question we ask is how is a harlot dressed? Have you ever seen a program on television in which they show a woman posing as a prostitute? If you have watched any of the police shows you see that. She may be a prostitute; she may be posing as one; she may be an undercover agent; she may be the hero; she may be the victim; she may be the bad guy, whatever. You have seen that and you know how they are dressed. You know that she is a prostitute before they ever tell you. Of course, they don't use that term; they use the term "hooker." Perhaps you have seen a television news broadcast which shows these women on the streets as they're out searching for business. All you have to do is look at the way they are dressed. The sad thing about it is that some Christian people dress the same way. Now, you don't want anybody to think that about you. You might wonder if people really think that about you. Yes, they do.

Here's an article from *McCall's* magazine. *McCall's* is not a Christian magazine. The editors are not trying to defend the Christian faith or propagate the Bible. Here's an article in *McCall's* magazine entitled "What Your Intimate Behavior Says about You." I'm going to read this. It may be offensive to some, but the words are not nearly as offensive as the way some people dress. We need to be honest and frank about this thing. It's not going to be vulgar, but plain. The writer says,

> "The female legs have also been the subject of considerable male interest as sexual signaling devices. The mere exposure of leg flesh has been sufficient to transmit sexual signals. Needless to say, the higher the exposure goes the more stimulating it becomes for the simple reason that it then approaches the primary genital zone."

That's what it's all about folks, and we had better wake up and realize it. He goes on to say, talking about the primary genital zone of the body,

> "The first way to accentuate is to employ articles of clothing which underline the nature of the organ hidden beneath them. For the female this means wearing trousers."

Now the fellow that wrote this is not a preacher. As a matter of fact, in this article he is telling you how to send sexual signals by the way you dress. He continues:

> "The way to emphasize the nature of the organs of the body is by wearing these clothing: trousers, shorts, or bathing costumes, that by their tightness reveal..."

This is what people think when they see you dressed this way. In the *Family Weekly* magazine they had a true or false question and answer section.

> "Question: What you communicate wordlessly has more effect on people than what you say?
>
> "Answer: This is true. ...
>
> "Question: People use clothes as a means of communicating with others?
>
> "Answer: True. Psychological studies at Britain's University of Newcastle have demonstrated that people use clothes to tell others what they want them to believe about them."

In other words the wearer is not trying to tell others what he is really like, but is trying to communicate his ideal self image, the kind of person he wishes he was. That's what these experts say. What you wear says something about you.

I know very well that not everybody who wears the items of clothing mentioned in the *McCall's* article has an immoral motive. Here's what I'm trying to get you to see: Whether you like it or not, this is what other people think. As a Christian, somebody interested in holiness, in winning people to Christ and getting people's minds off of sin, we need to go entirely the other way.

Whether you realize it or not, men look at certain portions of the body; and it doesn't matter whether you think that is good, bad, or otherwise, they are going to do it. And if you wear clothing that attracts attention to that, you are just helping them in their sin. That's why a dress, unless it's too tight, is better than pants; because a dress does not draw the attention to that part of the body that people look at and lust after.

I have a lot of other articles, but I have time for only one more. An article appeared in the *Richmond Times-Dispatch*, Richmond, Virginia, and the writer of the article was Anthony Surbony, a personnel manager for a large corporation. He had interviewed more than 14,000 men for jobs in the past years that he had been there. He said that the length of a person's hair tells a lot about him. Here's a man after 14,000 interviews. He said the left-wingers generally have long hair.

> "They reject self-discipline, authority, regulation, proven logic and reasoning. They are more easily swayed by popular opinions and propaganda. They tend to accept and do anything if somebody simply suggests it's a style. Many employers find that they tend to be more dreamers than doers, where the reverse is the trend on men with short hair. Why is it so? Mainly it is due to a self-centered personality."

I have been saying that for a long time.

There are certain things that I like about women that I don't like on men. I like for women to look nice, and it doesn't bother me at all to see a woman in front of a mirror primping and fixing her hair. But it just about makes me want to throw up to see a man do that, and I've seen men do that very thing, just like a woman.

I quote further from the article mentioned above. He said long hair indicates a self-centered personality.

> "The liberal left-winger seems to be more selfish and only aspire to goals that will benefit them individually, regardless of what it costs to others. They actually believe that long hair is beautiful on a man and they feel naked without it. They try to make up for lack of ability by attracting attention, or becoming a sex symbol. Long haired liberals also reject the basic hunter/warrior responsibilities of man. They seem to think that society should provide for them and that someone else should guarantee protection. Or else they don't really believe that there are any enemies. In fact, some tend to bow before enemies, hoping to gain friendship."

Men have lost the basic responsibility that God inbred into a human being to fight for what is his and to provide for what is his. Men reject that, and the first thing you know, they think the government owes them a living. They don't feel responsible to go out make a living any more. It all goes together. We must remember that this man is an expert in analyzing people.

When I am considering what kind of clothes to wear, I need to ask myself this question: What does it make other people think about me?

Predominately, what kind of people dress that way?

Here is the third question we need to ask: Predominately, what kind of people dress that way?

Do you think that a policeman who is going to be an undercover agent would dress like I am dressed? Do you think his hair would be as short as mine is? No, sir. Every policeman that I have ever seen or heard about in the last twenty years that became an undercover agent around the bars and gambling dens let his hair grow long, and wore sloppy, slouchy clothes, because that is the kind of people they are trying to catch. I don't want to look like that kind of person. It's not because I think I'm better than they are. It's because when Jesus saved me, He jerked me up out of that. That's what I used to be. I don't want to be that anymore. I don't want folks to think I've gone back to that.

See, here is the third question. Predominately, what kind of people wear the kind of clothes you are thinking of wearing? If it's the wrong kind, you surely don't want to identify yourself with it.

Must I use the arguments of the world to justify it?

Here is the fourth question: Must I use the arguments of the world to justify it?

> "Where is the wise? where is the scribe? where is the disputer of this world? hath not God made foolish the wisdom of this world?" (I Cor. 1:20).

> "That your faith should not stand in the wisdom of men, but in the power of God" (1 Cor. 2:5).

> "For this cause we also, since the day we heard it, do not cease to pray for you, and to desire that ye might be filled with the knowledge of his will in all wisdom and spiritual understanding" (Col. 1:9).

If you read these verses you find out there is a difference between the wisdom of the world and spiritual wisdom. A Christian is in trouble when he has to resort to the wisdom of the world to justify what he is doing. We ought to be able to use the wisdom of God. If I am going to defend my position I ought to be able to go to the Bible and use spiritual wisdom to do it. God help us if we have to use worldly wisdom to justify our clothing or actions.

Will it cause others to stumble?

Here is the fifth question: Will it cause others to stumble?

> "It is good neither to eat flesh, nor to drink wine, nor any thing whereby thy brother stumbleth, or is offended, or is made weak" (Rom. 14:21).

King David walked on his roof top. He was lazy; he was disobedient; he was out of God's will. But also he saw a woman washing herself. She was either out in a yard where everybody could see her, or else she was in the house without the curtains drawn. And she was equally guilty in that lusting experience. I know David was out of God's will and should have been out fighting the battles, because the Bible starts off that chapter by saying that it was the time that kings went out to war that David stayed at home. I know that was wrong, and she likewise was wrong in taking a bath where a man could see her.

What you do or what you wear, will it cause somebody to stumble? Now you might say the other fellow has to look out for himself. That is not what the Bible says. The Bible says, "It is good neither to eat flesh, nor to drink wine, nor any thing whereby thy brother stumbleth, or is offended, or is made weak." We are responsible.

[Note from Brother Cloud: Under the topic of causing others to stumble, we would mention the SLIT SKIRTS AND DRESSES that are so popular in the female fashion industry today. Certainly one purpose for this fashion is to tease men with the flashing effect that is created. It is strangely enticing. Even if the slit is below the knee the effect is very sensual. A few months ago we asked a group of young Bible college men if they were tempted sexually by slit skirts, and every one of them admitted that they are. This should speak volumes to Christian women and young ladies to avoid this immodest fashion.]

Conclusion

We have considered five good tests regarding clothing. Is it worn by the opposite sex? What does it make other people think of me? What kind of people dress that way? Must I use the argument of the world to defend it? Will it cause anybody else to stumble?

In closing, let me encourage you to have some Christian convictions, and let me make some strong suggestions to you about these.

Number one, make sure your convictions are biblically based. When you believe something is wrong, you had better have a good Bible reason for believing it. You ought to know where the Bible talks about that, and if you don't think you can remember it, write it down so you can show people. Have biblically based convictions, not just opinions.

Number two, when you have a conviction, be firm. Don't waver no matter what crowd you are with, no matter what environment you find yourself in. If it is wrong to wear a bathing suit walking down the street, it is wrong to wear one in the swimming pool. The water doesn't have anything to do with it. That is why you have to be careful about where you go swimming. Do you expose your body to the lustful thoughts of others? They are going to think it whether you like it or not. Be firm in your convictions.

Number three, be kind when you have convictions. Don't be a smart alek. When the time comes to express yourself, or to say no, or to give a reason, be kind about it. Learn your reasons, and know them, and don't be nervous, and don't be angry, and don't be snappy. Be kind about it.

Number four, don't act superior. Don't act like you are better than somebody else. That's the first charge they are going to make against you, I guarantee you. Anytime you ever have a conviction about anything, whether it be about music, or drinking liquor, others are going to say that you think you are better than they are. People have been saying that for centuries. That is not anything new. So don't act superior. Just let them know you aren't going to do that thing.

Number five, if you have to talk to somebody about these things deal with the heart first. All of this is a matter of the heart. You might get somebody straightened out on the matter of the clothes they ought to wear and they still be just as lost as they were before you met them. Before I talk to anybody about clothes or anything else, the first thing I want to know is what about the heart? Have you been saved? Acts 15:9. Has your heart been purified by faith? Romans 10:9. Have you believed in your heart that God raised Christ from the dead? The first thing I want to know is about the heart and salvation. All that I said here tonight applies to those who are saved. If you haven't been saved, it's not going to help you your soul one way or the other to change your clothes. It's not going to help at all. If Jesus does not live in your heart, that is your first need. You first have to come to Christ.

If you are saved it is still a matter of the heart. If I were talking to a Christian about this, the first thing I would want to talk to him about would be the heart. Is your heart right with God? If your heart's not right with God, you are not going to be able to understand any of this. You're going to resent every argument, and resent anybody even bringing up this discussion.

The Bible talks about the heart. Hebrews 10:22 --

> "Let us draw near with a true heart in full assurance of faith, having our hearts sprinkled from an evil conscience, and our bodies washed with pure water."

God is talking to Christian people there. And in verses 24 and 25,

> "And let us consider one another to provoke unto love and to good works: Not forsaking the assembling of ourselves together, as the manner of some is; but exhorting one

another: and so much the more, as ye see the day approaching."

Dressing properly is a matter of the heart.

A Study on Biblical Modesty

The following are key Bible passages on modesty that contain a wealth of instruction about the godly woman's attire. In examining these passages we will find that the principles therein have a direct bearing on the Christian's clothing. The principles and application of Scripture are important. Consider the issue of smoking. Even contemporary style preachers who do not touch clothing issues and who might claim the Bible does not speak directly to that issue avoid smoking. Why? The Bible does not say anything directly about smoking tobacco. Neither the words "smoking" nor "tobacco" are found in the Bible, but smoking is commonly avoided because of scriptural principles such as avoiding every appearance of evil and the Christian's body being the temple of the Holy Spirit. The same is true for avoiding marijuana and cocaine. Both of these drugs are popular in society at large, but the vast majority of evangelicals avoid them. It is not because marijuana or cocaine are directly addressed anywhere in Scripture; it is because of biblical principles such as avoiding every appearance of evil and being sober.

The principles of Scripture are to be applied to clothing just as they are to be applied to other areas of Christian living. In fact, we will see that the Bible not only gives principles that are applicable to clothing but it even directly addresses the issue.

"It is most curious then why dress and other appearance issues are so often a point of contention for Christians. Many who see the connection of the biblical principle of identity to other areas of life, somehow cannot see it in this one. The same person who would never use the world's profane speech will wear its equally profane clothes" (David Kidd, *The Fall and Rise of Christian Standards*).

1 Timothy 2:9-10

"In like manner also, that women adorn themselves in modest apparel, with shamefacedness and sobriety; not with broided hair, or gold, or pearls, or costly array; but (which becometh women professing godliness) with good works."

This is the key New Testament passage on female modesty. Note what it teaches us about the Christian woman's dress:

1. Her dress is to be modest ("adorn themselves in modest apparel," 1 Tim. 2:9).

This refers to a godly manner, a manner that is proper and fitting before God.

The Greek word translated **modest** ("kosmios") is also translated "of good behaviour" (1 Tim. 3:2). It means "decent and orderly" and describes "an inner self-control -- a spiritual 'radar' that tells a person what is good and proper" (*The Bible Exposition Commentary*). It refers to something that is becoming to a woman who professes godliness. The Christian woman should not wear anything that would be characterized as NOT of good behavior, as NOT becoming to a woman professing godliness.

2. Her dress is to be fitting for a woman displaying "shamefacedness" ("with shamefacedness," 1 Tim. 2:9).

"Shamefacedness" is translated from the Greek word "aidos," which "has the idea of downcast eyes" and means "bashfulness, i.e. (towards men), modesty or (towards God) awe" (Strong). It implies "a shrinking from trespassing the boundaries of propriety" (William Hendrickson, *New Testament Commentary*).

Shamefacedness is exactly the opposite of the cheeky, pert, saucy, impertinent, flippant, insubordinate attitude that the world seeks to develop in women today.

The shamefaced woman loves God in her heart and is committed to obeying His Word and this is reflected on her face.

A shamefaced Christian woman will not have the rebellious attitude that says, "Don't tell me how to dress; I will dress as I please!" She will not be stubborn and sassy. She will not say, "I don't care what some old-fashioned men say about how I dress; that is their problem; I'm not going to be a weirdo!"

3. Her dress is to be fitting for a woman displaying "sobriety" ("and sobriety," 1 Tim. 2:9).

"**Sobriety**" is translated from the Greek word *sophrosune*, which is also is translated "soberness" (Acts 26:25). It means "soundness of mind, self control" (Strong), "habitual inner self-government" (Trench), "the well-balanced state of mind arising from habitual self-restraint" (Ellicott), "moderation of the desires and passions, opposed to all that is frivolous and to all undue excitement of the passions" (Barnes).

Sobriety means not to be drunk, neither with alcoholic beverages, or drugs, or any other thing. Many professing Christian teenage girls and young women are drunk with the fashions and fads and ways of the world. They are drunk with television, and Hollywood movies and sensual magazines, and pop music. The Bible and the things of Christ do not excite them, but they are giddy over what some worldly movie star or pop singer is wearing and doing, and over the latest vain fashion or hair style or cosmetic.

Sobriety is the opposite of foolish, silly, flippant, careless, intoxicated, shallow, worldly, and vain.

We see from this passage that the Christian woman's modesty must come from the inside out. It comes from a sober and shamefaced spirit. It is a matter of the heart, which reminds us that it is not enough to set forth dress standards. Every effort must be made to educate the women so that they understand the biblical principles of modesty and know the reason for the church's standards, and every effort must be made to reach their hearts, to challenge them to surrender themselves wholly to Christ and to live for His glory.

4. Her dress is not be extravagant ("not with broided hair, or gold, or pearls, or costly array," 1 Tim. 2:9).

"Broided hair" refers to braiding the hair. This does not mean that the Christian woman should not take care of her hair; it is a warning against spending a great deal of time adorning herself in the manner of the world, of making this her focus in life. We agree with the Barnes commentary, which says: "It cannot be supposed that the mere braiding of the hair is forbidden, but only that careful attention to the manner of doing it, and to the ornaments usually worn in it, which characterized worldly females."

The mention of "gold, or pearls, or costly array" reminds us that it is God's will that the Christian woman refuse to display an extravagant, showy, worldly appearance. The goal of this world's godless fashion industry is to create a haughty, ostentatious, worldly-wise look, as well as a sexual look. The godly woman will reject such fashion and clothe herself and her daughters in "modest apparel." "It is not to be supposed that all use of gold or pearls, as articles of dress, is here forbidden; but the idea is that the Christian female is not to seek these as the adorning which she desires, or is not to imitate the world in these personal decorations. It may be a difficult question to settle how much ornament is allowable, and when the true line is passed. ... It is, that the true line is passed when more is thought of this external adorning, than of the ornament of the heart. Any external decoration which occupies the mind more than the virtues of the heart, and which engrosses the time and attention more, we may be certain is wrong" (Barnes).

5. Her dress should be fitting for a woman who adorns herself with good works (1 Tim. 2:10).

She should be known for her obedience to God and her service to Jesus Christ, rather than for her extravagance in dress or her devotion to sensuality and pleasure. "There is great beauty in this direction. Good works, or deeds of benevolence, eminently become a Christian female. The woman's nature seems to be adapted to the performance of all deeds demanding kindness, tenderness, and gentleness of feeling; of all that proceeds from pity, sympathy, and affection... God seems to have formed her mind for just such things, and in such things it occupies its appropriate sphere, rather than in seeking external adorning" (Barnes).

What, then, is a modest dress standard based on this important passage?

First, modest attire covers the body properly.

In the study on Genesis 3 we have seen that God completely clothed Adam and Eve in coats (Gen. 3:21). This is a good beginning point for modesty.

The woman should be covered decently so that the body is not improperly displayed in a sensual manner, because it would never be fitting for a godly, shamefaced, sober woman to dress in such fashion. It is obvious, then, that it is immodest to wear clothing that exposes the parts of the body that have particular sexual appeal. Isaiah 47:2 says that for a woman to bare her leg to show the thigh is nakedness. Thus immodest clothing would include short skirts, shorts, slit skirts, low blouses, short blouses that bare the midriff, deep V-necked dresses, backless dresses, halter tops, and any modern swimsuit.

Second, modest attire does not sensually accentuate the body.

Tight, clinging attire is as immodest as skimpy attire because the woman's figure is emphasized and accented, and the man's attention is directed to that which is forbidden outside of marriage. Men are strongly influenced sexually by the eye-gate and are attracted to the woman's curves. The immodest clothing industry understands these things and strives to dress women seductively rather than modestly.

It is important to understand that tight, form-fitting clothes can be just as sexually disturbing to a man as skimpy clothes.

In the book *For Women Only: What You Need to Know about the Inner Lives of Men*, Shaunti Feldhahn describes the following situation:

> "Another husband with a happy twenty-year marriage described another typical scenario: 'My wife and I recently went out to dinner at a nice restaurant with some friends. The hostess was extremely attractive and was WEARING FORM-FITTING CLOTHES THAT SHOWED OFF A GREAT FIGURE. For the rest of the night, it was impossible not to be aware that she was across the restaurant, walking around. Our group had a great time with our lovely wives, but I guarantee you that our wives didn't know that every man at that table was acutely aware of that woman's presence and was doing his utmost not to look in that direction" (p. 114).

In our survey of Christian men on the issue of women's dress we found that tight clothing is at least as much of a potential problem for men as skimpy clothing. Most of the men indicated that tight skirts and tight blouses and form-fitting jeans hold a "VERY great potential" for lust.

Consider the following statements:

> "I would say the number one problem is any garment that is form fitting, be it jeans, pants, skirt, dress, shirt, whatever. Anything that is tight, no matter how long it is, leaves nothing to the imagination, and that defeats the whole purpose of covering the skin in the first place!"

> "You don't even need to see skin; they provide all the curves." Another man said: "I would say the Number One problem is any garment that is form fitting, be it jeans, pants, skirt, dress, shirt, whatever. Anything that is tight,

no matter how long it is, leaves nothing to the imagination, and that defeats the whole purpose of covering the skin in the first place!"

"One thing I see in my church is tight clothing. Oh, it may very well be covering but it is revealing the shape in a woman. This can be even more tantalizing to a man."

"The point is that it is not merely the type of clothing that can trip a man up; rather it is the amount and the level of cling to the body."

Tight pants were designed by Calvin Klein, a bisexual fashion designer. When his super tight pants appeared in 1974, they sold 200,000 pairs in the first week.

Tights worn as pants were designed by Gianni Versace, a homosexual fashion designer who was murdered by a homosexual in 1997.

Godly women who understand what a temptation tight clothing is for men will be careful to avoid this type of attire.

Third, modest attire is not ostentatious or extravagant.

It is not the type of clothing that draws undue attention to the wearer or that makes the onlooker think that the wearer is improperly consumed with fashion. Modest attire will not draw undue attention to the woman's hair and clothes but will draw attention to her character. Those who see her will think about what a godly woman she is rather than what a "sexy" or "fancy" or "fashionable" one she is.

One man wrote: "When I see a woman in a store in town and she is dressed a certain conservative way, I always think, 'I bet she is a Christian.' It says a lot about the character of a woman when she shuns the styles of this world and walks in such a way that she wants to let people know that she is different."

Titus 2:3-5

"The aged women likewise, that they be in behaviour as becometh holiness, not false accusers, not given to much

wine, teachers of good things; that they may teach the young women to be sober, to love their husbands, to love their children, to be discreet, chaste, keepers at home, good, obedient to their own husbands, that the word of God be not blasphemed."

Consider some of the lessons of this important passage that touch on the issue of dress.

1. The older women are to be "in behaviour as becometh holiness."

This means that they live their lives in such a way as to bring glory to the Christ that they profess. People are always watching how we live; others are always affected. The elderly men and women must be examples to the younger. The older believers are mentioned first in Titus 2 because they should set the standard of morality in the churches.

The elderly women are to follow holy things rather than unholy and worldly. Elderly Christian women must be careful that they do not give themselves to evil things such as ungodly literature and television programs and movies and immodest dress. I recall an elderly woman who professed Christ who kept sensual romance magazines in her home, some of which even contained pornographic stories, and her grandchildren were corrupted by these. I know of other elderly believers who spend much of their time watching unwholesome television shows and Hollywood movies and are thus a very poor example for the youth. In his autobiography the blasphemous rock singer Marilyn Mansion described how he was influenced by wicked literature that was kept in the basement of his grandfather's house. This type of thing should not be once named among the saints.

The older woman might not be as physically attractive as the younger one, so she might think that it is not as important how she dresses since there is less chance of men lusting after her. This thinking errs in not recognizing that the older woman must be an example for the younger.

My own maternal grandmother, Julia Pollock, had a testimony of "behaviour as becometh holiness." She filled her last years with prayers and good works and holy living. I never saw her in any type of unfeminine or immodest attire, no matter what type of work she was doing. One of my favorite pictures is of her standing in her garden with a hoe in hand attired in a nice dress. When one would visit her, he would find absolutely no unwholesome literature; he would not find her watching unwholesome television programs. More often than not she would be sitting in her favorite chair crocheting something to give away or to sell so that she could give the proceeds to missions, or she would be reading her tear-stained Bible and praying for her children, grandchildren, pastor, neighbors, acquaintances, and missionaries. She had the habit of writing down some of her prayers, and it was wonderful to see God's answers. She was the first Christian I ever met who practiced fasting and prayer, and she witnessed some miraculous answers to prayer by this means. Though she had a serious heart condition for the final decade of her life and suffered greatly, she was cheerful and always had a good word of encouragement for her visitors and a challenge from the Scriptures. She and my grandfather had lived through the "great depression" and she always testified that God will take care of His own regardless of the situation. She loved Psalm 37:25, "I have been young, and now am old; yet have I not seen the righteous forsaken, nor his seed begging bread," and she often quoted it. She told of how the Lord miraculously provided for them when no jobs were available. I am confident that the earnest prayers of this godly woman had a large part in my conversion in the summer of 1973, because she exemplified "behaviour as becometh holiness." What a heritage and influence a godly older person can have!

2. The older women are to be "teachers of good things" (Titus 2:3).

The older Christian women are to teach the younger by example and by word. This is the older woman's chief ministry in the church, and yet in large numbers of cases it is not a ministry that is practiced effectively today.

The following is excerpted from the book *The Fall and Rise of Christian Standards* by David Kidd:

> "It is imperative to understanding the precise directive in this passage to acknowledge that the qualities of discretion and chastity are to be fostered in Christian 'young women.' This is not a suggestion, but a command. Furthermore, this mentoring is to take place within the church family. Such deportment is rapidly becoming extinct in the passion-driven culture which has swallowed up the vast majority of our youth. ...
>
> "Pastors bear a large share of the responsibility if they lack courage and conviction to proclaim the whole counsel of God to the sheep they are charged to nurture. Christian parents, also weakened by the relentless pressures of a society drunk with the liquor of licentiousness, have sacrificed chastity as a priority for their daughter's appearance, while desperately hoping that somehow she will retain it in her heart. Solomon describes this malady in Proverbs 11:22, 'As a jewel of gold in a swine's snout, so is a fair woman which is without discretion.'
>
> "The solution to the decay of these priceless qualities in young ladies is offered in a very simple church program to supplement the teaching of the Christian home. The older godly women are to teach the younger women principles of conduct befitting a Christian lady. THIS DOES NOT REQUIRE A FLAMBOYANT YOUTH LEADER OR A TIME-CONSUMING ADDITION TO THE CHURCH'S ALREADY OVERCROWDED SCHEDULE. Titus 2:3-5 can be fulfilled first by example, then by casual and homey discussions as ladies assume their God-given directive to

mentor younger women. Quite simply, it is to be a natural outgrowth of the church family's care for one another.

"Instead of a biblical model however, the church has opted for a secular one in which youth are portioned off into age-based groups, generally led by a young man, and provided with an entertainment-oriented method of instruction. This produces three undesirable outcomes:

"(1) By grouping those who lack spiritual maturity together, an environment of immaturity is created, working against the very goals Titus 2 establishes.

"(2) Youth are isolated from the very ones scripture says are to be their models and mentors.

"(3) The spiritually mature are denied access to those whom they are scripturally admonished to teach, by the very structure of church programs which are supposed to be facilitating that same biblical instruction!

"This is not to imply that there are no positive outcomes, but that the process we are following is not conducive to the results scripture says we are to seek. Age-based grouping does not originate from biblical patterns but from secular, educational psychology. That fact alone does not make it wrong, but where it conflicts with what we find in scripture, we who profess to follow scripture should do so, regardless of what the 'experts' say.

"*A return to biblically-based standards of modesty, decency and propriety, along with the methods to achieve them, are a life or death priority for the 21st century church and family*. We must nurture and protect the virtues of innocence and purity, in ourselves and our children, lest we lose their hearts to a culture which is eager to fatten itself on their spiritually decaying remains" (David Kidd, *The Fall and Rise of Christian Standards*).

3. The qualities of a young Christian woman who pleases the Lord are given in Titus 2:4-5.

After first addressing the older women, the apostle next turns his attention to the younger women and what they are to be taught and how they are to live.

The young women are to be "**sober**" and "**discreet**" (Titus 2:4).

Both of these words are translated from the Greek word "sophron," which means sober-minded, self-controlled, spiritually-disciplined. It is translated "temperate" in Titus 2:2. It means the same thing as "sobriety" in 1 Timothy 2:9.

Sober is the opposite of being foolish and careless and vain. It refers to a woman who is wise, who is mindful of eternal values, morally vigilant, not carried away by the vanities of this world, not devoted to the things to which unregenerate women are devoted.

It refers to a woman who is not caught up, for example, in worshipping and lusting after and imitating Hollywood and pop stars.

It refers to a woman who is not giddy after the sensual fads and products of the fashion industry.

It refers to a woman who is not inordinately consumed with physical beauty, recognizing that beauty without godliness is of no value before God (Prov. 11:22).

If the words "sober" and "discreet" are so similar in meaning, why does God's word use both in the same context? The answer is that both are used by way of emphasis, and the reason this is so emphasized is because of the woman's weaker nature and her greater susceptibility to deception (1 Tim. 2:14). Eve sinned because she did not maintain vigilance and because she assumed that she was capable of making decisions that should have been left to her husband. She was not sober; she was carried away by her emotions and by her natural senses and by her imagination (Gen. 3:6).

The Christian woman must be sober and discreet by what she allows herself to think about, by what she reads, by what she watches, by the conversations she has. Some women have left their husbands and children because they were not careful in these matters; they allowed their minds to be filled with foolish and evil thoughts, and they were eventually carried away by such things.

The woman must also be sober and discreet by what she wears. Any style that is not characterized by attendance to spiritual and moral vigilance, anything that is morally loose or questionable, is not discreet.

The young women are also to be "**chaste**" (Titus 2:5).

This is translated from the Greek word "hagnos," which means "clean, innocent, modest" (Strong). It is also translated "clear" (2 Cor. 7:11) and "pure" (Phil. 4:8). It is used to describe a "chaste virgin" (2 Cor. 11:2).

The Holy Spirit is emphasizing the moral purity that should characterize a Christian wife and mother. In some ways, women set the standard for morality, both in a church and in society at large. If women are not chaste, everything around them becomes impure. They set the standard in the home as they rear the children.

Christian women must therefore be absolutely chaste in the way they dress.

One of the first things God did after Adam and Eve sinned was clothe them properly and decently (Gen. 3:21). Because of the fallen condition of man's heart (Jer. 17:9), women must act, dress, and carry themselves in such a manner that they do not entice men sexually.

The Christian woman is responsible not to cause others to stumble (Rom. 14:21).

The young women are also to be "**good**" (Titus 2:5).

This is translated from the Greek word "agathos," which is the word most commonly translated "good"; it is also translated "benefit" (Phile. 14) and "well" (Rom. 2:7).

This describes the woman's life overall. She is to be a good woman whose life is filled with good works. Consider Dorcas, who was "full of good works" (Acts 9:36). That was her testimony; it was the chief characteristic of her life, and this should be the testimony of every female Christian.

"Good" also refers to the woman's spirit (1 Pet. 3:4). "It may also have, as some think, a more particular sense; one of a meek and yet cheerful spirit and temper, not sullen nor bitter; not taunting nor fretting and galling any; not of a trouble-some or jarring disposition, uneasy in herself and to those about her; but of a good nature and pleasing conversation, and likewise helpful by her advice and pains" (Matthew Henry).

A good Christian woman will be very careful about what she wears and will be sensitive to the Holy Spirit's guidance and reproof.

4. The Christian women must live in this manner so "that the word of God be not blasphemed" (Titus 2:5).

The reason why the Christian woman should live the kind of life described in this passage is to glorify her Lord and Saviour. If she lives in sensuality and rebellion and follows the standards of the world rather than the standards of Scripture, she causes the Word of God to be blasphemed. The unsaved are looking at churches and at professing Christians and they judge God and His Word by what they see.

Today, in all too many cases, the world sees no difference between the way that Christians live and the way that they live. Lost people are thus given a reason to say, "Those Christians do not live any different than we do; there must not be anything to Christianity."

1 Corinthians 6:19-20

"Flee fornication. Every sin that a man doeth is without the body; but he that committeth fornication sinneth against his own body. What? know ye not that your body is the temple of the Holy Ghost which is in you, which ye

have of God, and ye are not your own? For ye are bought with a price: therefore glorify God in your body, and in your spirit, which are God's."

This is a foundational passage on modesty in Christian dress, because it reveals two of the chief motives for dressing properly, which are to glorify God and to avoid fornication. The believer that lives for the glory of God and for moral purity is willing to sacrifice his or her own desires. He does not try to justify his every action in order to have his own way.

Notice that the believer is to glorify God both in body and in spirit. The argument that God looks on the heart so it doesn't matter how we dress ignores this fact. The Bible teaches that God is concerned by what we do with our bodies just as surely as He is concerned by the condition of our hearts. Since God has said that the body is to be clothed and since He did not accept the fashion that Adam and Eve invented after their fall and since he has said many other things on this issue in Scripture, this means that God is concerned about what we wear.

Fornication is something that is committed both with the body and the spirit. Jesus said, "But I say unto you, That whosoever looketh on a woman to lust after her hath committed adultery with her already in his heart" (Matthew 5:28). Fornicating lust is a powerful motivation in society, and the fashion industry feeds on this lust. For the Christian that wants to glorify God, there is no choice but to avoid every type of fashion that is associated with sexual lust, whether it is clothing that is too short or too low or too tight or too teasing or whatever.

1 Peter 3:1-5

"Likewise, ye wives, be in subjection to your own husbands; that, if any obey not the word, they also may without the word be won by the conversation of the wives; while they behold your chaste conversation coupled with fear. Whose adorning let it not be that outward adorning

of plaiting the hair, and of wearing of gold, or of putting on of apparel; but let it be the hidden man of the heart, in that which is not corruptible, even the ornament of a meek and quiet spirit, which is in the sight of God of great price. For after this manner in the old time the holy women also, who trusted in God, adorned themselves, being in subjection unto their own husbands."

Some of the major lessons from this passage in reference to modest attire are as follows:

1. The most important characteristic in a Christian woman is her godly spirit.

She is to be in subjection to authority. She is to exhibit a meek and quiet spirit. She is to be a woman who trusts in God and fears God and has her attention directed to pleasing Him.

This is the woman's greatest power in this world, the power even to win a rebellious husband to Christ. The godly woman's influence is great, and it is therefore worthwhile for a woman to cultivate that meek and godly lifestyle that is described in this passage. The carnal and worldly Christian woman also has a great influence, of course, but it is not toward godliness and righteousness.

The woman who manifests the qualities described in this passage is a woman who is easily taught in God's Word and led by the Holy Spirit. She is humble and receives reproof in a godly manner.

The woman who fears God and cultivates godliness in "the hidden man of the heart" is a woman who wants to reflect this in her manner of dress. When she learns that men are sexually enticed by certain types of clothing, she will not have the attitude, "Well, that is their problem!"

2. The Christian woman's conversation or manner of living is to be chaste.

As we have seen, the word "**chaste**" is translated from the Greek word "hagnos" and it is elsewhere translated "pure" (Phil. 4:8; Jam. 3:17; 1 John 3:3). It is used to describe a "chaste virgin" (2 Cor. 11:2).

When applied to dress, the Christian woman must avoid any style that is not chaste and morally pure. This would include anything that shows her off in a lascivious manner; anything that exposes her in an indecent way; anything that is tight so that her figure is emphasized in a sensual way; anything that exposes her chest (which belongs only to her husband, Proverbs 5:19), or her thigh, which is said to be nakedness (Isa. 47:2).

3. The Christian woman should not focus on plaiting the hair, and wearing gold, and putting on of apparel.

This does not mean it is wrong for a woman to fix her hair or wear any jewelry. Elsewhere in Scripture we see that the godly woman "maketh herself coverings of tapestry" (Prov. 31:22). Peter is simply contrasting the ways of the world with the ways of Christ. The worldly woman focuses on the physical, while the spiritual woman focuses on the things of God. While the spiritual woman tries to dress in a proper and respectable and feminine manner, this is not the main thing in her life. The main thing for her is pleasing the Lord and cultivating godliness. She puts on apparel, but she does not put on immodest apparel and putting on apparel is not one of her chief loves in life. She takes care of her hair and might wear some inconspicuous item of jewelry, but she does not do so ostentatiously or in a sexy manner and such things do not captivate her heart or characterize her testimony.

1 Corinthians 6:12-13; 10:23-24

"**All things are lawful unto me, but all things are not expedient: all things are lawful for me, but I will not be brought under the power of any. Meats for the belly, and** the belly for meats: but God shall destroy both it and them. Now the body is not for fornication, but for the Lord; and the Lord for the body" (1 Cor. 6:12-13).

"All things are lawful for me, but all things are not expedient: all things are lawful for me, but all things edify not. Let no man seek his own, but every man another's wealth" (1 Cor. 10:23-24).

These verses are frequently misused by those who desire liberty to fulfill their carnal desires. They would have us believe that the apostle Paul is saying that the Christian has liberty to wear immodest clothing, watch indecent movies, go to the beach half naked, listen to sensual rock music, etc.

Is that what Paul meant by the statement "all things are lawful unto me"? By no means! Obviously there are limitations to the Christian's liberty. I have counted 88 specific rules that the believer is to obey in the book of Ephesians alone, and that is the book that says we are saved by grace and not of works!

When Paul said all things are lawful to him he meant that the Christian has been set free by the blood of Christ, free from the wages of sin, free from the condemnation of the law, free from the ceremonies of the Mosaic covenant, but *not* free to sin or to disobey the Bible or to do anything that is not expedient or edifying or glorifying to Christ.

Paul explains himself clearly in both passages. In 1 Corinthians 6:12-13 he uses the example of eating meat. In 1 Corinthians 10:23-28 he uses the example of eating things that have been offered to idols. In all such things, the Christian is free. There are no dietary restrictions for the New Testament Christian as there were under the Mosaic Law. We do not have to fear idols; we know they are nothing. This is the type of thing Paul is referring to in 1 Corinthians 6 and 10, if we allow him to explain himself rather than attempt to put some strange meaning upon his words that would fill the Bible with contradiction.

Paul addresses the same thing in Romans 14. The Christian is free from laws about eating and keeping holy days (Rom. 14:2-6). We are not to judge one another in these matters or any other matter on which the New Testament is silent. Obviously this does not mean we cannot judge anything at all and that we are free to do whatever we please. Such a philosophy is contrary to the entire tenor of the New Testament and is an appalling perversion of these passages.

FOUR TESTS FOR CHRISTIAN ACTIVITIES

Far from saying that all things are lawful in the Christian life, in 1 Corinthians Paul gives four tests to determine whether the Christian should allow a certain thing in his life: First, does it bring me under its power? Second, is it expedient? Third, does it edify? Fourth, does it help or does it hinder my fellow man, does it cause my fellow man to stumble?

These are tests that are to be applied not to clearly sinful things that are already forbidden in God's Word, but to things the Bible does not specifically address. If these tests were to be applied to things commonly allowed in the world of contemporary Christianity it would put a quick stop to many practices.

Immodest female fashions, for one, fail every one of these tests. First of all, immodest dress can bring a Christian under its power. The female world at large is indeed under the power of worldly fashion. They are giddy with the thought of the latest style, cosmetic, hair fashion, etc. There is a seductive power in these things because of the fallen nature. Second, immodest dress is not expedient or edifying, because it is not holy and godly and it increases sexual lust in this world. Further, immodest dress does cause men to stumble and hinders their Christian lives. Of the 150 Christian men who have written to me on this subject just in the past week, every one said that immodest clothing presented a serious temptation to them. Clothing, such as shorts and bathing

64

suits and short skirts and tight jeans, *does* hinder our fellow man by putting before him a temptation to sin in his thought life.

The apostle Paul had such a low view of "personal liberty" that he was willing to forego the eating of meat for the rest of his life if he thought that such eating would harm his fellow man. "Wherefore, if meat make my brother to offend, I will eat no flesh while the world standeth, lest I make my brother to offend" (1 Cor. 8:13).

Paul did not have the idea that he was in this world to live as he pleased.

Paul's attitude is in direct contrast to the view of Christian liberty that reigns in the world of contemporary Christianity. Those who are consumed with their "liberty" will not forego even highly questionable things such as rock music and sexy dress styles for the sake of glorifying Christ and edifying their fellow man. When confronted with such things, they become puffed up and lash out against straw men such as "legalism" and "lack of love."

Romans 14:22-23

"Hast thou faith? have it to thyself before God. Happy is he that condemneth not himself in that thing which he alloweth. And he that doubteth is damned if he eat, because he eateth not of faith: for whatsoever is not of faith is sin."

There is a simple principle in this passage that applies to dress and to any other thing in the Christian life: if it is questionable don't do it. If you have a doubt about it and if you cannot approach it by faith and as a matter of clear conscience, then it is best to leave it alone. This is a helpful standard in the area of dress. If it a clothing style is questionable and borderline it should be rejected. If you have to say, "Well, I'm just not sure if this is acceptable," it has failed the biblical test.

Isaiah 3:16-24

"Moreover the LORD saith, Because the daughters of Zion are haughty, and walk with stretched forth necks and wanton eyes, walking and mincing as they go, and making a tinkling with their feet: Therefore the Lord will smite with a scab the crown of the head of the daughters of Zion, and the LORD will discover their secret parts. In that day the Lord will take away the bravery of their tinkling ornaments about their feet, and their cauls, and their round tires like the moon, the chains, and the bracelets, and the mufflers, the bonnets, and the ornaments of the legs, and the headbands, and the tablets, and the earrings, the rings, and nose jewels, the changeable suits of apparel, and the mantles, and the wimples, and the crisping pins, the glasses, and the fine linen, and the hoods, and the vails. And it shall come to pass, that instead of sweet smell there shall be stink; and instead of a girdle a rent; and instead of well set hair baldness; and instead of a stomacher a girding of sackcloth; and burning instead of beauty."**

In this passage God reproved the women of Isaiah's day, not only for how they dressed but also for how they carried themselves. We have seen in the New Testament that true modesty is first a matter of the heart, and that is evident in this Old Testament passage, as well.

1. These women were haughty (Isa. 3:16).

This is the very opposite of "shamefacedness" (1 Tim. 2:9). The modern fashion industry appeals to the pride of life and encourages women to cast off their natural feminine timidity, to be brazen and hard and proud.

2. They had "*wanton eyes*" (Isa. 3:16)

Wanton eyes describes the woman who walks after the lust of the eyes, who is sensual, who seeks to entrap men by her physical beauty. The Hebrew word translated "wanton" is used only in this verse, and it means "to ogle, i.e. blink coquettishly" (Strong). It refers to "making the eyes to glance about" (Jamieson, Fausset, Brown). "Their eyes are wanton, deceiving (so the word is); with their amorous glances they draw men into their snares" (Matthew Henry).

"Wanton eyes" is the opposite of "shamefacedness and sobriety" (1 Tim. 2:9), the opposite of "discreet, chaste" (Titus 2:4, 5), the opposite of "a meek and quiet spirit" (1 Peter. 3:4).

3. They walked in a mincing manner (Isa. 3:16).

They walked so as to draw attention to themselves and to cause men to notice them. They walked in an enticing manner. They walked like Hollywood movie stars and fashion models.

4. They made a tinkling with their feet (Isa. 3:16).

It appears that they wore little bells or chains or ankle bracelets that would make a sound as they walked so as to more assuredly draw attention to themselves. They wore *tinkling ornaments about their feet"* (Isa. 3:18). Modern fashion, too, uses many devices to draw attention to the wearer. This is done by the brazen cut of the clothes, by plunging necklines and short skirts and bare midriffs, or by teasing slits, or by taps on the shoes, or by very loud or clashing colors, or by high heels, or by tight calf-high boots, or by rips in the clothing, etc. It is also done by the immodest use of jewelry, cosmetics, and perfume.

5. They were devoted to every sort of fashion (Isa. 3:18-23).

The list of attire and ornaments described here is simply amazing. They had ornaments for their feet, their arms, their hands, their legs, their necks, their heads, their hair, their ears, their noses, you name it! Their hearts were obviously devoted to fashion of every sort, and they spent a large percentage of their time *thinking about* women's fashion and *shopping* for fashion and *adorning* themselves in fashion, and *showing* themselves off.

This is the opposite of the exhortation of 1 Timothy 2:9-10, which says women are to adorn themselves modestly, "not with broided hair, or gold, or pearls, or costly array," and that of 1 Peter 3:3, which says the godly woman's adorning should not be "that outward adorning of plaiting the hair, and of wearing of gold, or of putting on of apparel."

Proverbs 7:6-23

"For at the window of my house I looked through my casement, and beheld among the simple ones, I discerned among the youths, a young man void of understanding, passing through the street near her corner; and he went the way to her house, in the twilight, in the evening, in the black and dark night: And, behold, there met him a woman with the attire of an harlot, and subtil of heart. (She is loud and stubborn; her feet abide not in her house: Now is she without, now in the streets, and lieth in wait at every corner.) So she caught him, and kissed him, and with an impudent face said unto him, I have peace offerings with me; this day have I payed my vows. Therefore came I forth to meet thee, diligently to seek thy face, and I have found thee. I have decked my bed with coverings of tapestry, with carved works, with fine linen of Egypt. I have perfumed my bed with myrrh, aloes, and cinnamon. Come, let us take our fill of love until the morning: let us solace ourselves with loves. For the goodman is not at home, he is gone a long journey: He hath taken a bag of money with him, and will come home at the day appointed. With her much fair speech she caused him to yield, with the flattering of her lips she forced him. He goeth after her straightway, as an ox goeth to the slaughter, or as a fool to the correction of the stocks; till a dart strike through his liver; as a bird hasteth to the snare, and knoweth not that it is for his life."

This passage describes the immoral woman, and she is in direct contrast to what God requires of the modest woman in every way.

They are different in where they go. The strange woman is not afraid of going out "in the black and dark night" (Prov. 7:9). Her "feet abide not in her house; now is she without, now in the streets" (Prov. 7:11-12). The modest woman, on the other hand, is cautious about where she goes and when she goes and with whom she goes; she avoids going to places where moral temptations lurk; she avoids being alone with a man other than her husband and close relatives; she avoids situations that could place her in the way of moral harm.

They are different in their attire (Prov. 7:10). The immoral woman has "the attire of an harlot"--skimpy, tight, suggestive, seductive, tantalizing--to draw attention to herself sexually and to lure men to her on that basis. The modest woman, on the other hand, is clothed in such a way so as NOT to draw men's attention to her in a sexual manner. The immoral woman wants to catch a man with her body, whereas the modest woman wants to catch a man with her godliness.

They are different in spirit (Prov. 7:10-11). The immoral woman is "subtil of heart ... loud and stubborn." The modest woman has "a meek and quiet spirit" (1 Pet. 3:4).

They are different in countenance (Prov. 7:13). The immoral woman has "an impudent face." The modest woman, on the other hand, is "shamefaced" (1 Tim. 2:9).

They are different in their approach to religion. The strange woman makes religious offerings and attends to religious duties (Prov. 7:14), but her heart is far from God; she may go to church but she is a hypocrite, because her secret life is wicked. The modest woman, on the other hand, serves God from the heart. She is the same person in the dark of night as she is in the light of day.

They are different in their definition of love. The strange woman confuses love with lust, thinking that "love" is mere romance and the fulfillment of sexual desire regardless of one's marital status (Prov. 7:18). This is the Hollywood, the rock & roll definition of love. The modest woman, on the other hand, knows that genuine love is godly commitment in marriage. True love is keeping God's commandments (1 John 5:3).

They are also different in the way they look at life. The strange woman lives only for the moment; she does not look at the end of things but only at the beginning. She does not think about God's judgment but only about the pleasure of sin (Prov. 7:22-23). The modest woman, on the other hand, knows that sin is pleasurable only for a short season and she focuses her attention rather on the eternal than the mere temporal (Heb. 11:24-26).

Proverbs 22:6
"Train up a child in the way he should go: and when he is old, he will not depart from it."

This verse reminds us that training in modesty best begins in childhood. Many married women in Bible-believing churches did not have an opportunity to grow up in a godly Christian home and were not taught how to be modest when they were young, but now they have the opportunity to provide such a home for the next generation. This is a great blessing as well as a large responsibility.

The best time to teach a girl how to dress modestly is when she is a toddler. When she reaches teenage years she will be habituated to dressing in a feminine and modest manner and will not feel strange wearing a nice dress. She will also know how to be decent wearing a dress, because she learned it from her mother (and hopefully grandmother, aunts, etc.) from childhood.

One of our granddaughters is three years old, and her mother dresses her in nice dresses all of the time except when she is bathing and sleeping or getting ready for bed and is in her pajamas. She is learning how to sit properly in a dress. She is learning that her brother wears pants but she wears dresses, because she is different. My earnest prayer is that she will never turn aside from this modest and lovely and scriptural way of dressing.

Of course, the key is not merely dressing a child properly but teaching her why she is dressed that way, instilling in her the Bible principles of modesty throughout her childhood, and praying that she will be saved and take these principles to heart because she wants to please the Lord. Female fashions change constantly, and the Christian woman must learn how to apply Bible principles to whatever comes along.

Beware of the fashion industry. It is trying to sexualize children from a young age, and parents and grandparents must refuse to purchase the trash that is being offered. The following warning is very timely:

> "It was a hot summer's day in 2002 when I decided to buy sandals for our 4- and 6-year-old daughters. I never anticipated our retail excursion would prove to be so educational. We're talking sandals, now. Plain, ordinary sandals, the kind every one of us grew up in. But after going to eleven different stores I still couldn't find anything even remotely suitable. Why? Because every pair of sandals I found--every single pair--had high heels.
>
> "High heels for a 4-year-old? How can a child run and jump and play wearing high heels? I'll tell you the answer: She can't. Apparently, girls' sandals aren't meant for running and jumping and playing. They're meant to make little girls look like tarts. ...
>
> "It amazes me that 40 years after the sexual revolution that was supposed to 'free' women from the 'oppression' of men, we find ourselves teaching our daughters that their only worth is in looking slutty. Boys don't respect girls anymore because girls don't require and demand it. And it all starts by buying 4-year-olds high-heeled sandals and Bratz dolls.
>
> "So, who is at fault for pre-sexualizing our kids? Sure, we can blame a lot of things. Society. The fashion industry. Hollywood. Public schools. Pick one.

"But what it boils down to is you, the parent, allowing it. Yes, allowing it. ...

"I've heard some parents say they can't 'stop' pre-sexualization because kids will learn it in school or from peers. Many parents feel victimized, swept helplessly along the tide of society and unable to do anything about it. Hogwash. It's parents who are permitting inappropriate clothing, toys, posters and music into their homes" ("Sexy Six Year Olds," *WorldNetDaily*, May 31, 2008).

It is equally important for parents to beware of the toy industry. When our kids were growing up we never allowed Barbie Dolls or any other such thing in our house. Now there are Bratz Dolls (franchised by MGM) and a slew of other sexualized toys.

The following timely warning is from a concerned grandmother:

"I attend a fundamental church but have noticed that some parents don't seem to have any qualms about allowing their young daughters to play with Barbie dolls. And even Polly Pocket dolls are becoming more immodest in their clothing. Also the accessories for both Barbie and Polly Pocket dolls promote a worldly look and a worldly lifestyle. ... I believe that these kinds of dolls are too immodest for girls of any age to play with, much less little girls around the ages of 4 and 5. They definitely promote the wrong message and wrong focus in a young girl's life.

Worldliness and the Christian's Dress

The issue of dress is intimately associated with the issue of worldliness. The following passages contain practical instruction on separation from the world that applies to Christian dress standards.

1 John 2:15-17 and James 4:4

"Love not the world, neither the things that are in the world. If any man love the world, the love of the Father is not in him. For all that is in the world, the lust of the flesh, and the lust of the eyes, and the pride of life, is not of the Father, but is of the world. And the world passeth away, and the lust thereof: but he that doeth the will of God abideth for ever" (1 John 2:15-17).

"Ye adulterers and adulteresses, know ye not that the friendship of the world is enmity with God? whosoever therefore will be a friend of the world is the enemy of God" (James 4:4).

This present world system is wicked and in rebellion to God. It was created by rebellious men beginning with Cain, who rejected God's Word and "went out from the presence of the LORD" (Gen. 4:16). Cain's son Enoch, the father of the first polygamist, built the first city and he and his children established the first culture (Gen. 4:17-24). Thus the world system is not the Christian's friend. It is the enemy of God and the person who loves this wicked world does not love God and, in fact, is His enemy. Those are strong words, but that is what the Bible teaches. It is important that we not be deceived in this manner, because Christianity at large is at home in this world and does not preach separation from the world. I call it "rock and roll Christianity."

What is it about the world that we are to separate from? When God's Word says to love not the world it is referring to the evil things of the world rather than to the things that God created. It is referring to "the lust of the flesh, and the lust of the eyes, and the pride of life."

This is a perfect description of the modern fashion industry. It is geared to showing off the body in a sensual way and fulfilling the lust of the flesh and of the eyes and the pride of life. The very concept of **BEING "COOL,"** which is so important to young people, has to do with something that excites the lust of the flesh, the lust of the eyes, and the pride of life.

One web site says that ripped jeans are "cool" and then goes on to describe why they are cool. It is because they "sport the 'I don't care' look" and are "a mark of rebellion." Further, they were made popular by rock stars (Brittney Spears, we are told, wore them to her wedding) and are thus hip. Ripped jeans also "make the wearer stand out in the crowd and get noticed." Thus this youthful web site admits that "cool" refers to something that appeals to the lust of the flesh and the pride of life.

One of the most powerful things in human society is the lust of the eyes, and the most powerful lust is that of sexuality. Men, in particular, have an endless propensity to lust after women, and this is why Jesus said: "Ye have heard that it was said by them of old time, Thou shalt not commit adultery: But I say unto you, That whosoever looketh on a woman to lust after her hath committed adultery with her already in his heart" (Mat. 5:27-28). The fashion industry appeals directly and continually to this powerful lust by enticing women to dress in a skimpy, revealing, tight, tantalizing manner that attracts the man's lust.

The pride of life is another powerful thing in society, and the fashion industry caters to this as well. Men want to be thought of as cultured (or uncultured, whatever the case may be) and proper (as defined by one's crowd) and respectable (or disrespectable), etc., and the fashion industry excites this lust and feeds upon it. Ralph Lauren's line of clothing, for example, is said to have "taste and snobbism." This is the pride of life, and it is a sinful motivation that God condemns. The opposite of the pride of life is humility, which the world ridicules.

God plainly and solemnly forbids His people to participate in these things that characterize the fallen world. *The believer has a clear and serious choice; either he can follow the world or he can follow Christ, but he cannot do both.* If he loves the world, he does not love the true and living God and in fact becomes God's enemy.

The Christian's dress must avoid anything that smacks of the lust of the eyes, and the lust of the flesh, and the pride of life. The Christian must analyze his clothing carefully and apply these high standards.

The lust of the eyes refers particularly to clothing that is sensual and sexy, that which feeds the fallen desires associated with fornication and adultery and lasciviousness, that which would cause men to lust adulterously because of what it reveals and how it is cut.

The pride of life refers to dress styles that exalt self and draw attention to me in such a manner that I become proud. Label consciousness has a lot to do with the pride of life. What motivates people to buy clothes that are outrageously expensive when similar clothes can be purchased cheaply? It is the label and the desire to be thought of as cool and "hip" and "in" and "smart." It is the pride of life.

Romans 12:1-2

"I beseech you therefore, brethren, by the mercies of God, that ye present your bodies a living sacrifice, holy, acceptable unto God, which is your reasonable service. And be not conformed to this world: but be ye transformed by the renewing of your mind, that ye may prove what is that good, and acceptable, and perfect, will of God."

We see in this passage that knowing God's will requires separation from the world. Salvation is a free gift, but finding the will of God after salvation is prize to be sought. It requires zealous Christian living. It is impossible to pattern one's life after the world and also know the will of God, and this exposes the error of the "rock and roll Christian" philosophy that wants to get as close to the world as possible while still thinking of itself as Christian. This passage makes it very clear that separation from the world is not an option for the dedicated Christian!

Separation from the world is described in terms of not being conformed to it. It means not allowing the world to shape me into its mold, its image, its way of thinking, its pattern of living; not allowing it to shape me by its philosophy, fashions, entertainment, etc. We have seen that the world is characterized by the lust of the eyes, and the lust of the flesh, and the pride of life, and God's people must not allow themselves to be conformed to this in any area of life.

We see that the world is evangelistic. It is not content to "do its thing" and leave Christians alone. It evangelizes its philosophy and ways and fashions, putting pressure upon Christians to conform. The world is one of the Bible believer's three great enemies, the other two being the flesh and the Devil. God's people must have the conviction and backbone to resist the world's enticements and pressures. We have a far superior manner of lifestyle in God's Word, and we must not be ashamed of it.

The way to avoid being conformed to the world is to be transformed by the renewing of the mind. This is accomplished by the Scripture, which is "quick, and powerful, and sharper than any twoedged sword" (Hebrews 4:12). By reading and studying and memorizing the Bible and sitting under its preaching and teaching, the Christian learns to think God's way and thus learns to prove the perfect will of God in every area of his or her life. By the Word of God the Christian gets spiritual discernment so that he can weigh issues and come out on the side of God's will. He thereby gains the wisdom necessary to understand the wiles of the devil and to discern the difference between the things of the

Spirit and the things of the flesh. The carnal Christian, on the other hand, remains a babe in his understanding of the Bible and thus lacks wisdom and spiritual understanding (Heb. 5:5-11-14). Those who are strong in God's Word "have their senses exercised to discern both good and evil" (Heb. 5:14). In this way the strong Christian can determine the issues of clothing wisely. He or she will not be deceived by the fashion industry and will not dress according to what is cool and hip but according to what is godly.

Another important part of not being conformed to the world is to avoid letting the world into our homes and churches. I have often been amazed at how Christian parents let their children watch Hollywood movies and play video games that feature indecently dressed people. We must understand that such things are not innocent, not even PG-rated and even most G-rated ones, and they have a great influence toward worldliness. If you are accustomed to watching such movies, notice, the next time you watch one, how the females are dressed and ask yourself if that is the way you want your daughters to dress. Christian parents need to go through their homes and analyze everything with an eye for whether it tends to encourage them and their children to godliness and modesty or to worldliness. Are there seductively-dressed Barbie Dolls? Are there unwholesome teen magazines? Are there video games and movie DVDs and music CDs that need to be tossed?

Titus 2:12-15

"For the grace of God that bringeth salvation hath appeared to all men, teaching us that, denying ungodliness and worldly lusts, we should live soberly, righteously, and godly, in this present world; looking for that blessed hope, and the glorious appearing of the great God and our Saviour Jesus Christ; Who gave himself for us, that he might redeem us from all iniquity, and purify unto himself a peculiar people, zealous of good works. These things

speak, and exhort, and rebuke with all authority. Let no man despise thee."

We see in this important passage that grace teaches us to live godly. Any teaching of "grace" that results in careless living is not the true grace of God. Grace is not license. It is not legalism or "Phariseeism" for a blood-washed Christian to seek to live godly in this present world and for a New Testament church to preach godly living. While the believer is not saved *by* good works, he is saved *unto* good works (Eph. 2:8-10). The believer's works do not add to salvation; they are the *product of* and *demonstration of* salvation. The believer does not work *in order to be saved* or to assist in his salvation; he works *because he has been saved*. The believer's works are not his own works; they are the work of God in Him (Gal. 2:20). He works because Jesus Christ lives in him and changes, renews, and motivates him. He works because he has been redeemed by a great price and he is thankful to his Saviour and desires to please Him.

This passage in Titus 2 describes a very strict level of Christian living.

1. The believer is to deny ungodliness and worldly lusts.

This refers to all forms of evil, both internal and external. "The phrase 'worldly lusts,' refers to all improper desires pertaining to this life--the desire of wealth, pleasure, honour, sensual indulgence. It refers to such passions as the men of this world are prone to, and would include all those things which cannot be indulged in with a proper reference to the world to come" (Barnes). This reminds us that sin is still present in the believer, but it is to be denied.

2. The believer is to live soberly, righteously, and godly.

Putting away evil is not enough; we must also *put on* godliness. Living *soberly* has to do with our duty to ourselves, "to live in control of our evil propensities and passions." Living *righteously* has to do with our duty toward our fellowman; treating others in a just manner. Living *godly* has to do with our duty toward God, pleasing Him in all that we do.

3. The believer is to live with his eyes on the next life ("in this present world," Titus 2:12).

He knows that this present life is short and that the next life is eternal. He can therefore endure hardships and temptations more easily because he knows that these things are temporal.

It is the will of Christ that His people be peculiar. The word "peculiar" is translated from the Greek word "periousios," which means "beyond usual, special" (Strong). God's people are to be different from the world. "Peculiar" is defined in this context as people who are "redeemed from all iniquity" and "zealous of good works." That certainly does not characterize the world. The world is not redeemed. It might be religious but it does not care about pleasing the God of the Bible in all matters. The Bible-believing Christian, though, does live to please God and this makes him peculiar. Those who are afraid of standing out in the crowd in this world will never please God. We have to realize that Christ paid a great price to redeem us and He therefore owns us and has the right to tell us how to live. "For ye are bought with a price: therefore glorify God in your body, and in your spirit, which are God's" (1 Cor. 6:20). We are not at home in this world; we are pilgrims merely journeying through this foreign land on the way to our eternal home with the Lord (Heb. 11:13-16), and we must not act like we are citizens of this wicked world.

This exhortation has many applications to the Christian's clothing. Our clothing must not be associated with ungodliness and worldly lusts of any sort. Thus any fashion that is immodest, indecent, and "sexy" is out of bounds. Our clothing must be characterized by righteousness and godliness and be fitting for a peculiar people who have been saved and who are citizens of another country and are ambassadors of the Lord of that country (2 Cor. 5:20). We must not be afraid of being different. We must not let the world set the agenda for our dress but we must show the world a better standard, that is "an heavenly."

Ephesians 5:11

"And have no fellowship with the unfruitful works of darkness, but rather reprove them."

Note that the works of darkness are unfruitful. The believer's chief desire should be to please his Master and to bring forth fruit for His glory. Anything that is unfruitful should be avoided. Jesus said, "I am the true vine, and my Father is the husbandman. Every branch in me that beareth not fruit he taketh away: and every branch that beareth fruit, he purgeth it, that it may bring forth more fruit. ... YE HAVE NOT CHOSEN ME, BUT I HAVE CHOSEN YOU, AND ORDAINED YOU, THAT YE SHOULD GO AND BRING FORTH FRUIT, and that your fruit should remain: that whatsoever ye shall ask of the Father in my name, he may give it you" (John 15:1-2, 16). The fruit of the Spirit "is in all goodness and righteousness and truth" (Eph. 5:9), and everything that is not goodness, righteousness, and truth must be rejected.

This verse has far-reaching applications for the Christian's clothing. "Works of darkness" is an apt description of the modern fashion industry. Unisex fashion is a work of darkness that was created by the homosexual-controlled clothing industry in direct rebellion to God. So is the punk style with its philosophy of anarchy. Any style of clothing that is immodest in any way and that is designed to be "sexy" in public is a work of darkness.

James 1:27

"Pure religion and undefiled before God and the Father is this, To visit the fatherless and widows in their affliction, and to keep himself unspotted from the world."

We see that pure religion before God is not only to care for the needy but also to keep oneself unspotted from the world. This is a high standard of separation. A spot is a small thing. To be unspotted is to keep oneself from every type of evil and unrighteousness. If this is taken as one's standard for Christian clothing, it would be the highest type of standard. It is better to be too careful in this matter than not careful enough.

1 Peter 1:14-17

"As obedient children, not fashioning yourselves according to the former lusts in your ignorance. But as he which hath called you is holy, so be ye holy in all manner of conversation; because it is written, Be ye holy; for I am holy. And if ye call on the Father, who without respect of persons judgeth according to every man's work, pass the time of your sojourning here in fear."

In this passage the believer is exhorted to live differently than he lived before he was saved. This is one of the Scriptures that motivated me to cut my hair and stop visiting bars and throw away my rock & roll record collection and quit attending Hollywood movie theaters and quit smoking and many other things after I was saved in 1973. I cut my hair because I did not want to be identified any longer with the things I was identified with as a lost person.

Notice the high standard of Christian living that is described in this passage. "As he which hath called you is holy, so be ye holy in all manner of conversation." The standard is to be holy like the thrice holy God and to be holy in all manner of conversation. No believer reaches that perfect standard in this life (1 John 1:8), but this is the goal of the Christian who loves the Lord. To be holy in all manner of conversation is to be holy in every area of one's life, in spirit, in body, in dress, in music, in reading, in entertainment, you name it. Again we see that it is not legalism or "Phariseeism" for the born-again Christian to seek to live the very holiest life possible in this world in order to please the God who saved him.

Observe that the Christian is to live in the fear of God. Some wrongly teach that the only proper motive for Christian living is love for God, but that is not true. Love for God is indeed a good and high motivation for Christian living, but there are many proper motives for godly Christian living, and one of them is fear. The judgment seat of Christ is a great motivator for godly Christian living. If I know that I will stand before God and give an account for my earthly life, I will be more careful about how I live. I will be more concerned about pleasing God than pleasing people. A young Christian person who understands this will be like Daniel who "purposed in his heart that he would not defile himself" (Dan. 1:8). He will be like Moses who chose "to suffer affliction with the people of God, than to enjoy the pleasures of sin for a season; esteeming the reproach of Christ greater riches than the treasures in Egypt: for he had respect unto the recompence of the reward" (Heb. 11:24-26). The Christian lady who walks in the fear of God does not care if her clothing style is not perfectly fashionable and that she stands out in the ungodly crowd. She lives to please the God before whom she will be judged rather than the fickle and foolish crowd in this world.

Note that it is possible for a believer to continue to live as he did before he was saved to some extent. Otherwise we would not be exhorted to put away the former lusts. The child of God has a choice about how he or she lives in his world, and the wise choice is to live a holy life in all manner of conversation.

2 Corinthians 6:14-18

"Be ye not unequally yoked together with unbelievers: for what fellowship hath righteousness with unrighteousness? and what communion hath light with darkness? And what concord hath Christ with Belial? or

what part hath he that believeth with an infidel? And what agreement hath the temple of God with idols? for ye are the temple of the living God; as God hath said, I will dwell in them, and walk in them; and I will be their God, and they shall be my people. Wherefore come out from among them, and be ye separate, saith the Lord, and touch not the unclean thing; and I will receive you, And will be a Father unto you, and ye shall be my sons and daughters, saith the Lord Almighty"

This is another clear scriptural commandment to separate from the evil of this world. Paul asks several rhetorical questions, such as, "what fellowship hath righteousness with unrighteousness?" The answer in every case is that there is no such fellowship. Light doesn't dwell with darkness and Christ is not in concord with the Devil and the believer has no part with an infidel and the temple of God has no agreement with idols. These are opposites and they should never be joined together.

The point Paul is making is that God's people should be different from the world because we are a heavenly people and the world is earthly, sensual, devilish. In applying this to how we dress, it is obvious that it is not God's will for His people to attire themselves in fashions that are designed by the world for its lascivious and rebellious purposes. "No honest evaluation of Paul's instruction to the Corinthians on living lives separate from the world can leave the objective believer with an understanding that Christians may rightfully adapt to fads and styles which epitomize a godless culture and defy biblical principles" (Kidd, *The Fall and Rise of Christian Standards*, p. 106).

It is not the unsaved people themselves that we are to avoid so much as their sinful ways. The emphasis in this passage is on unrighteousness, deeds of darkness, devilishness, and idolatry. The Lord Jesus did not avoid the unsaved, nor did His apostles. Jesus was a friend of sinners, but He never sinned with sinners; He never participated in anything that

83

was unrighteous or rebellious or idolatrous. In this sense He was "holy, harmless, undefiled, separate from sinners" (Heb. 7:26). The apostle Paul spent much of his time with the unsaved trying to win them to Christ, but he would rather have died than to have participated in anything that was unrighteous. At all times and in all things Paul was "under the law to Christ" (1 Cor. 9:21). The believer does not win the lost by adopting their dress styles and party ways but by living a holy and separated lifestyle and lovingly preaching the gospel to the unsaved from that separated position. This is the example we see in the Gospel and the book of Acts.

It is important to observe that something is not wrong for the Christian merely because unsaved people do it. It is wrong when unsaved people do it in order to satisfy the lusts of the flesh, the lust of the eyes, and the pride of life, when they do it as an act of sin and rebellion. Unsaved people do many things that are not wrong in themselves. It is the things that the unsaved do that are unrighteous, satanic, and idolatrous that Paul is warning about. Consider the man's suit and a baseball style cap and penny loafers. Unsaved men wear these, but that does not make them wrong. A suit or a baseball cap or a loafer shoe is not directly associated with evil or rebellion or idolatry. If the cap has some evil slogan on it or if the suit is cut in some sort of style that identifies it with homosexuality, then it becomes identified with evil. Something that the unsaved do or wear is not wrong unless it is identified with sin and rebellion and idolatry, and when God's people encounter such things they must separate from it.

Note again that it is God's express will that His people be different and peculiar from the world. This is what so many professing Christians seem to be deathly afraid of, but it is commanded in Scripture. We are to be separate, peculiar, different, set apart. We must bear His stamp. We must stand out from the crowd because we are walking by heaven's light. When God's people are no longer peculiar to the world they have compromised the Word of God. We must fear God more than man. We must be more concerned about pleasing God than people. We must not draw back from bearing Christ's reproach in this wicked world. He said, "Whosoever therefore shall be ashamed of me and of my words in this adulterous and sinful generation; of him also shall the Son of man be ashamed, when he cometh in the glory of his Father with the holy angels" (Mk. 8:38). Paul said that if we deny him, he also will deny us (2 Tim. 2:12).

Note from this passage that God will receive us only if we separate from the wicked and unclean things. This exposes the gross error of the "rock & roll Christian" philosophy that says we should identify with the world to reach the world. This is an impossible task because when we identify with the wicked things of the world, with its lascivious and rebellious dress styles and sensual music, for example, we displease God and become His enemy. How can we reach the world for Christ if we are the enemies of God!

Philippians 2:15-16

"That ye may be blameless and harmless, the sons of God, without rebuke, in the midst of a crooked and perverse nation, among whom ye shine as lights in the world; holding forth the word of life; that I may rejoice in the day of Christ, that I have not run in vain, neither laboured in vain."

Here again we see the character of the world, that it is dark and crooked and perverse. It is at enmity with God. It is in open rebellion against the Creator. It cares nothing for His Law. Ever since Cain went out from the presence of the Lord and his children built a culture without God (Genesis 4:16-24), this world system has been godless. It has its religion, of course, but it is a lie. The word "crooked" is translated from the Greek word "skolios," which is also translated "froward" (1 Pet. 2:18) and "untoward" (Acts 2:40). The word "perverse" is translated from the Greek word "distrepho" and it means to distort or to corrupt. It is translated "to pervert" in Luke 23:2 and "to turn away from" in Acts 13:8. These are apt descriptions of this world system. Compared to God's perfect Law it is crooked and strange and wrong.

We also see again that God's people are to be different from the world. We are in the world but we are not of the world; we are heavenly people on a pilgrimage through a strange land. We are sons of God whereas the unsaved are children of the Devil. He is the "god of this world" (2 Cor. 4:4). This is why God's people have in the past sung, "This world is not my home; I'm just a passin' through"!

Note that the power of the believer's testimony and his evangelistic ministry is in being blameless and harmless and not living like the perverse world around him. This is how we shine as lights in a dark world, not by being like the world but by being different from the world! We hold forth the word of life from a position of being separated and peculiar. The "rock & roll Christian" culture would have us believe that the power of the believer's testimony is in identifying with the world so that we can gain their ear for the gospel. This is contrary to every passage we have looked at. It is contrary to the example of Jesus Christ and of His apostles. Some will doubtless argue that many are coming to Christ through "rock & roll" evangelism, but what is happening, in reality, is that the world is being won to a worldly type of Christianity. If you use the world to win the world, you win the world to the world.

The Christian's clothing, then, must be distinctively different and must be set apart from anything that is worldly. We must avoid any style that is identified with the world's crooked and perverse ways.

Note that believers are exhorted to be "without rebuke." This reminds us of the judgment seat of Christ where our lives will be examined. We must be more concerned about pleasing God in this world and the next than about fitting in with this present foolish world.

1 Thessalonians 5:22

"Abstain from all appearance of evil."

This verse is far reaching and has many applications to the Christian's clothing. God's people should never be identified with evil in any sense. If a clothing style is identified with rebellion against God's laws, with anarchy, with sexual freedom, with blasphemy, with idolatry, with moral decadence, or with any other evil it should not be worn by a Christian.

For example, the world's dance music has influenced fashion dramatically in the past few decades. Rock, punk, and rap have created or popularized such fashions as long hair on men, tight front-zippered masculine jeans on women, hip-hugging jeans on women, low-slung baggy jeans, torn jeans, the mini-skirt, the bare midriff, multiple piercings, and tattoos. God's people should not be identified with such things, because they are associated with evil and rebellion.

Hindu women wear red for worship. That is their religious identity. When you see a group of women all attired in red in India or Nepal, you know they are Hindus and are doing some sort of worship. Thus when people come to Christ in that part of the world they often avoid wearing red so as not to be identified with idolatry. One new believer recently told my wife that she had given away her red saris, because that was her "old life."

2 Timothy 2:22

"Flee also youthful lusts: but follow righteousness, faith, charity, peace, with them that call on the Lord out of a pure heart."

This verse contains important instruction about separation from the world.

First, separation is a protection matter. Timothy was exhorted to "flee" youthful lusts. This reminds us that sinful lusts are dangerous. They are to be fled like as from a poisonous snake or a roaring lion. The Christian who lives in sin will be chastened by God and if he hardens his heart he can commit the sin unto death (1 Jn. 5:16-17). The Christian who lives in sin loses the opportunity he could have used to walk with Christ and to do His perfect will in this world and to bear fruit to His glory. The Christian who lives in sin wastes the precious hours of this life on vanity. He is backslidden and makes wrong and foolish decisions because he lacks spiritual wisdom and is not seeking God's face. He can marry the wrong person and take the wrong job and get the wrong education and make the wrong friends and spend his money the wrong way and enter the wrong contractual agreements and join the wrong church and many other things that have serious consequences. Thus Paul warns Timothy to flee youthful lusts.

The child of God that is wise will heed this and will follow it in every area of life, including dress. As we have seen, youthful lusts have a lot to do with fashion. Fueling youthful lusts is one of the chief engines of the fashion industry.

Second, we see in this verse that separation is a heart matter. Paul reminded Timothy of those who call on the Lord out of a pure heart. These are the people that Timothy was exhorted to spend his time with. Those whose hearts are right with the Lord are willing to be corrected and for them the call to separate from the world is not too difficult.

When I was converted in the summer of 1973 I had hair down past my shoulders and I liked it. I used to get long rides when I hitchhiked and I thought it was because I looked like Jesus, with my long hair and beard. (You have seen pictures of the "hippy Jesus," I am sure.) After I was converted, the Lord began to deal with me about my hair, and I began to cut it off a bit at a time. After a few months I was out one evening on visitation with a man who was discipling me and we knocked on the door of a house and were invited in by an elderly woman. My friend had begun to talk to her about the Lord when she interrupted him and said, "I don't want to hear you talk to me about the Lord with that long haired man here representing the church." I was taken back and I could have done many things at that point. I could have said, "Look, lady, you should have seen my hair a couple of months ago," or, "Hey, my hair is really none of your business," or, "Who are you to talk to me about hair when you don't even go to church," or, "Haven't you ever heard how that Jesus said, 'Judge not that ye be not judged!'" But by the grace of God I said, "I am sorry that I have offended you; I will go to the barber shop tomorrow and get it cut short," and that is exactly what I did and I haven't had a problem with it since. If the believer's heart is right with the Lord he is open to correction and reproof and is willing to hear even the "hard" things of Scripture such as separation from the world.

My wife grew up in a non-Christian home and was saved as a teenager and began to attend a Baptist church in Alaska. She didn't know anything about the Bible, but she loved her Saviour and wanted to please Him. In her last year of high school she moved to Washington State and attended a small school. She was accustomed to wearing short dresses, because that was the style and she didn't know that there was anything wrong with it. One of her teachers, knowing that she was a Christian, took her aside and spoke a few words to her about having a dress with the proper hem length so it would be decent, and she took his counsel and bought a modest dress. She could have told him that she didn't have much money for clothes and she was trying her best to do right and if what she wore didn't please him he could go jump in a lake because it was none of his business! She could have charged him with being a "legalist" and determined never to attend a church that had that type of position. The reason she did not do any of these things is that her heart was right with the Lord and she was genuinely seeking His will.

One lady wrote to me and made the following important comment about how it came about that she learned to dress modestly. "When I desired to understand the holiness of God, to fear the Lord and to separate from the world, my increased love for Him affected everything I did, even how I dressed. It was and always will be a heart issue."

Third, this verse teaches us that separation is a replacement matter. Timothy was not only instructed to flee youthful lusts but also to "follow righteousness, faith, charity, peace, with them that call on the Lord out of a pure heart." The positive side of separation teaches me to replace what I give up. When I give up worldly music I need to replace it with sacred music. When I give up worldly friends I need to replace them with godly ones. When I give up worldly literature I need to replace it with wholesome literature. If I try to separate from worldly things and do not replace them with godly ones a vacuum is created and it will not be long before I will backslide from my decision to separate. Many times young people get excited during a special meeting or at a youth camp and they determine to give up rock music and other things, but they are not careful to cultivate godly influences in its place and they soon return to their old ways.

It is not necessary to replace each worldly activity with some Christian version of that same activity, but it is necessary to replace worldly activities with zealous service to the Lord in general by developing a fruitful daily Bible study and devotional time and a regular prayer closet and with faithful church attendance and with fellowship with serious and godly Christians and with evangelism and such. It has rightly been said that "an idle mind is the Devil's workshop." The way to make spiritual progress in the Christian life and to stay separated from evil things is to fill one's life with godly service to the Lord.

Pants and the Christian Woman

One of the battlegrounds of standards for Christian dress in North America and many other places is the issue of pants on women, and though this has been touched on previously I want to address it more thoroughly in this section. I do not believe this is a complex issue. There are two simple Bible reasons why we are convinced that Christian women should not wear pants.

The Unisex Issue

First, female pants are a unisex fashion statement and play a central role in the modern unisex movement. This was explained in the chapter "Bible Guidelines for Clothing" by Bruce Lackey, but it bears repeating.

Deuteronomy 22:5 forbids women to wear that which pertains to the man.

> "The woman shall not wear that which pertaineth unto a man, neither shall a man put on a woman's garment: for all that do so are abomination unto the LORD thy God."

Those who argue that pants are suitable attire on Christian women try to discredit the use of this verse by claiming that it is part of the Law that was done away. While we know that the Law of Moses is not the Christian's Law, it does contain lessons for Christian living. In 1 Corinthians 10 Paul recounts many things from the Pentateuch and concludes, "Now all these things happened unto them for ensamples: and they are written for our admonition, upon whom the ends of the world are come" (1 Cor. 10:11).

While Deuteronomy 22:5 is a part of the Law of Moses and the New Testament believer is not under that Law and lives by a higher law, the Law of the Spirit, it is also true that Deuteronomy 22:5 contains a moral principle that is written for our admonition. The principle is that there is to be a clear distinction between how men and women dress.

Paul emphasized this in 1 Corinthians 14:34 when he said, "Let your women keep silence in the churches: for it is not permitted unto them to speak; but they are commanded to be under obedience, as also saith the law." Thus, according to Paul, the Law of Moses does speak directly to Christian living in the matter of the created difference between male and female.

Another way that some try to discredit the use of Deuteronomy 22:5 is by saying that if we follow this verse today we must also follow Deuteronomy 22:9-11, which is in the same passage and which says:

> "Thou shalt not sow thy vineyard with divers seeds: lest the fruit of thy seed which thou hast sown, and the fruit of thy vineyard, be defiled. Thou shalt not plow with an ox and an ass together. Thou shalt not wear a garment of divers sorts, as of woollen and linen together."

Though we do not obey these commandments in the material realm today, we still must follow the principle that they teach in the spiritual realm. By giving these commands God was teaching Israel the principle of separation. They were not to mix seed or types of cloth because by so doing they were illustrating in their daily lives the fact that they were to make a distinction between good and evil. Such laws were designed to teach them "that ye may put difference between holy and unholy, and between unclean and clean" (Lev. 10:10). Deuteronomy 22:9-11, then, reminds the New Testament Christian that he is to separate from everything that is evil and wrong before the Lord (Mat. 6:24; 2 Cor. 6:14-17; 1 John 2:15-16, etc.).

Commentators of past centuries, who were not prejudiced one way or the other by the debate on modern fashions, held that the teaching of Deuteronomy 22:5 is applicable to the Christian life.

The footnotes in the **Geneva Bible (1560)** said: "The woman shall not wear that which pertaineth unto a man, neither shall a man put on a woman's garment: for all that do so are abomination unto the LORD thy God. For that alters the order of nature, and shows that you despise God."

Matthew Poole (1624-1679) said: "Now this is forbidden, partly for decency sake, that men might not confound, nor seem to confound, those sexes which God hath distinguished, that all appearance of evil might be avoided, such change of garments carrying a manifest umbrage or sign of softness and effeminacy in the man, of arrogance and impudency in the woman, of lightness and petulancy in both; and partly to cut off all suspicions and occasions of evil, which this practice opens a wide door unto."

Matthew Henry (1662-1714) said: "The distinction of sexes by the apparel is to be kept up, for the preservation of our own and our neighbour's chastity, De. 22:5. Nature itself teaches that a difference be made between them in their hair (1 Cor. 11:14), and by the same rule in their clothes, which therefore ought not to be confounded, either in ordinary wear or occasionally."

John Gill (1697-1771) said: "The woman shall not wear that which pertaineth unto a man, … It being very unseemly and impudent, and contrary to the modesty of her sex. … neither shall a man put on a woman's garment; which would betray effeminacy and softness unbecoming men, and would lead the way to many impurities, by giving an opportunity of mixing with women, and so to commit fornication and adultery with them; to prevent which and to preserve chastity this law seems to be made; and since in nature a difference of sexes is made, it is proper and necessary that this should be known by difference of dress, or otherwise many evils might follow; and this precept is agreeable to the law and light of nature…"

Adam Clarke (1762-1832) said: "It is, however, a very good general precept understood literally, and applies particularly to those countries where the dress alone distinguishes between the male and the female. The close-shaved gentleman may at any time appear like a woman in the female dress, and the woman appear as a man in the male's attire. Were this to be tolerated in society, it would produce the greatest confusion."

Albert Barnes (1789-1870) wrote: "The distinction between the sexes is natural and divinely established, and cannot be neglected without indecorum and consequent danger to purity (compare 1 Cor. 11:3-15)."

Jamieson, Fausset, Brown (1864) said: "They were properly forbidden; for the adoption of the habiliments of the one sex by the other is an outrage on decency, obliterates the distinctions of nature by fostering softness and effeminacy in the man, impudence and boldness in the woman as well as levity and hypocrisy in both; and, in short, it opens the door to an influx of so many evils that all who wear the dress of another sex are pronounced 'an abomination unto the Lord.'"

Perhaps you have observed that many of these older commentators cross referenced the principle of Deuteronomy 22:5 with that of 1 Corinthians 11 where Paul teaches that the woman and the man are to maintain a difference in appearance. "Doth not even nature itself teach you, that, if a man have long hair, it is a shame unto him? But if a woman have long hair, it is a glory to her: for her hair is given her for a covering" (1 Cor. 11:14-15).

Paul says the distinction in appearance should be maintained because of the created order and the different roles that the man and the woman were designed to fill.

> "For a man indeed ought not to cover his head, forasmuch as he is the image and glory of God: but the woman is the glory of the man. For the man is not of the woman; but the woman of the man. Neither was the man created for the woman; but the woman for the man" (1 Cor. 11:7-9).

In the beginning God made man and woman for different roles on earth.

> "So God created man in his own image, in the image of God created he him; MALE AND FEMALE CREATED HE THEM" (Gen. 1:27).

Thus both the Old and the New Testaments teach that it is God's will for the man and the woman to dress distinctively. One woman made the following important observation:

> "People seem to be playing 'pick-n-choose' with Old Testament verses. They want the twenty-third Psalm, the hundredth Psalm, and all the OT verses that won't affect their lifestyle, but then they try to explain away any OT verse that would have any effect on how they live. Well, 2 Timothy 3:16 says, 'ALL SCRIPTURE is given by inspiration of God, and IS PROFITABLE for doctrine, for reproof, for correction, for instruction in righteousness" (http://www.momof9splace.com/modesty.html).

The history of female pants in Western society

Since the created order has not changed and God has not changed, it is obvious that the modern unisex movement is in open and wicked rebellion against the Almighty and His Word. The Christian should have nothing whatsoever to do with such a movement and such a philosophy.

That pants on women is a unisex fashion is obvious when one examines the history of when and why women began to wear pants in Western culture. Pants on women arose from a social revolution in the twentieth century wherein women were fighting for their "rights" and struggling to be equal to men. Their pants are a feminist and a unisex statement.

The saying, "Who wears the pants in the family" illustrates the fact that pants were traditionally male attire and the woman who wore them assumed a masculine role. The universal symbols distinguishing the male from the female (a stick man in pants and a stick woman in a dress), and still used on the doors of public toilets to this day, arose from the fact that pants were traditionally male attire.

The article "Pants for Women" on the secular web site BookRags.com observes that "pants for women emerged" from "the feminist movement."

William Nicholson, in the book *Clothing the Universal Language*, observed that in the 1920s "wearing slacks to the office or to a park was still out of the question, and any female who appeared on a formal occasion in a trouser's suit was assumed to be a Bohemian eccentric and probably a lesbian."

It was in the late 1930s prior to World War II that pants on women began to be a fashion statement, and it began in Hollywood, which has always pushed the moral boundaries. Katherine Hepburn and Marlene Dietrich were at the forefront of this.

> "When diva film star Marlene Dietrich appeared in slacks with flared bottoms in her United States debut film *Morocco* in 1930, she signaled the emergence of women's pants from sportswear to high fashion. Wearing them both in films and private life, she popularized the pants look" ("Pants for Women," www.bookrags.com).

Pants still were not commonly accepted among women in society at large, though. That did not happen until after World War II. Women's slacks and capris grew slightly in popularity in the 1950s, but it was not until the 1960s that pants on women came into their own through the rock & roll revolution. "[T]he jeans and pants of the 1960's and the 1970's were serious gestures toward total sexual equality" (Nicholson).

> "[Unisex fashions appeared in the 1960s.] Both men and women wore blue jeans, 'hipsters' and close fitting pants with zip fly fronts. The spirit of this latest association of pants with social and sexual liberation can be seen in Alice Walker's novel *The Color Purple* (1982), in which the social

victory of the heroine culminates in her opening of a unisex jeans shop" ("Pants for Women").

The *Illustrated Encyclopedia of Costume and Fashion* makes the same observation on the history of pants on women:

> "The real pants revolution came in the 1960s, with unisex fashions, though even at this time women wearing pants were often refused entry to restaurants and the whole subject was one of heated debate. By the 1970s rules and social attitudes had relaxed and pants of many lengths and styles had become an acceptable part of female dress for both casual and formal attire."

This secular book admits that the growth in the popularity of pants on females in Western culture was part and parcel with the sexual revolution and the unisex phenomenon, both of which are an affront to the God of the Bible. Social attitudes had to be changed, and that occurred through the onslaught of the rebellious rock & role culture.

The modern unisex society knows that there is a major difference between the male and female, of course, but it emphasizes only the physical difference and the result is lust and immorality.

One woman wisely observed:

> "Oh there will always be a difference in gender, because there HAS to be. But now the emphasis is not on the beauty of a girl's femininity (which brings out the masculinity in a man). NOW the emphasis in the difference in BODY PARTS! There is no longer the striking difference between a beautiful woman in feminine attire, long pretty hair, and a masculine man that practices chivalry. (Put a real feminine woman around a man and see how chivalrous he becomes.) Now the difference is emphasized in her physical body difference, which leads to lust and a degradation of womanhood (and manhood too). A feminine woman is in her rightful place of an elevated position. But as soon as she steps down off her pedestal to

wear pants and be 'equal' to a man, it drags everybody down, which is exactly what Satan wants. The devil is still whispering in Eve's ear to destroy mankind" (http://www.momof9splace.com/modesty.html).

Why would the godly woman want to be identified with a fashion that is so intimately associated with a movement and philosophy that is in rebellion against God's created order?

Many men of God have observed that the popularizing of pants-wearing by women in the past 40 years has gone hand-in-hand with a shocking decline in female modesty. One pastor wrote:

> "I believe it leads to a breakdown of the sexes, causes immorality and contributes to homosexuality. Pants cause a woman to act masculine. Women today do not know how to sit like a lady or to act modestly because of their pants. They have lost the ability to act modestly. They no longer bend at the knees, but they bend at the waist, exposing their chest in even a modest garment. They do not sit with their knees together and the ankles crossed."

Another wrote:

> "Are we godlier today than our grandparent's generation? I think not! They were scandalized by women who wore pants and swimsuits and mini-skirts. Today, those things are commonly accepted among believers and even in churches."

Another man said:

> "I am 68 years old and have been married to a wonderful, modest lady for 49 years. I am appalled at how so many women dress even in church. My mother is 88 years old and worked in the cotton fields along side my father back when we did it all by hand. I've never seen my mother or either of my grandmothers in pants or shorts and they all worked in the fields. I have never seen any of the women who raised me in any of the items that you mentioned. I thank God for the example they were to me. By the way, they all washed their clothes by hand and I never saw any

women's undergarments hanging out on the clothes line for all that passed by to look at. This proves that their modesty went far deeper than what they put on their bodies. It was in their hearts."

While we can't turn the clock back to that bygone era, God's people can hold to the old Bible paths and reject the dictates of this shallow, lascivious, and rebellious age.

The Modesty Issue

The second reason why we are convinced that Christian women should not wear pants is that they are not modest.

Advertisements for women's jeans leave no doubt about the fact that pants on women are immodest. On what part of the body do these advertisements focus? They focus on the way that men respond lustfully to jeans' accentuation of the woman's figure in general and a most sexually stimulating part of her body in particular. Jeans are portrayed as the party girl fashion, as something worldly guys love because of what they can see.

In the book *How to Marry the Man of Your Choice* by Margaret Kent (New York: Warner Books, 1987), this secular author instructs women in how to use clothing to "manipulate men." She says, "Don't let the power of clothing pass you by, for it can be a major asset in attracting men. ... stir his sexual imagination without satisfying his curiosity about your body" (pp. 29, 32). As for pants on women, the author states that "jeans are likely to get a positive response because they are snug and outline the body; they also represent casualness" (p. 36).

The Christian female authors of the book "Dress: The Heart of the Matter," give the following testimony:

> "Should women wear pants? No! In fact, wearing pants accents or draws attention to the pelvic and hip area of the lady, areas only her husband should see. A dress does not draw attention to this area unless it is too tight and

formfitting" (Shirley Starr and Lori Waltemyer, *Dress: The Heart of the Matter*, p. 37).

We would add that a dress, even if tight and formfitting, doesn't draw attention to the pelvic area as any type of pants do.

Cathy Corle, in her book *What in the World Should I Wear?*, describes the following enlightening scene:

> "A friend of mine told me that her decision to restrict her wardrobe to dresses and skirts came as a result of a ladies' class. All the arguments and reasons that could be given were unheeded until the lady who was speaking said, 'Let me just demonstrate something to you.' She asked the ladies in the audience to close their eyes momentarily. She held up a large picture of a woman in an attractive, modest feminine skirt and blouse. She asked the ladies to open their eyes. Then she inquired, 'What is the primary focal point to this picture? Where did your eyes first fall naturally?' The audience agreed that their eyes were first drawn to the face of the woman in the picture. She once again asked the ladies to close their eyes. When they opened their eyes they were looking at a large poster of a woman in a sport shirt and hip-hugger blue jeans with snaps down the fly. She asked, 'Now, be honest with yourselves, and tell me where your eyes first fell naturally when you looked at this picture?' Many of the ladies in the crowd were surprised to find that most people's eyes first focused upon the hips and crotch area that were so vividly emphasized before they ever noticed the woman's face. If this happened in a crowd of ladies, how much more would it be true of men? For my friend, Joetta, this was all the 'evidence' that was needed."

One lady wrote to me in response to my quest for testimonies from women who have gotten a conviction against wearing pants and said,

> "I never have felt comfortable in wearing pants. ... Anything that brought attention to certain parts of my body bothered me."

Another lady wrote,

> "Pants only attract the wrong attention, and the only way
> to change your attitude is surrender, to desire to please the
> Lord more than yourself and the world."

It is obvious to me, as a man, that pants emphasize the woman's figure in a sensual way and are therefore not modest. *In my estimation, a woman in pants is never as modest and as unquestionably feminine as she is in a proper dress.*

In the section of this book on "Questions Answered on the Issue of Christian Dress" we have answered many of the questions and challenges that come up on the subject of pants on women, such as the following:

"I wear pants because there are many things I can't do in a modest manner if I wear a dress."

"I only wear feminine pants."

"I only wear modest pants."

"Preachers who preach against pants are mean-spirited and they just want to dictate how I dress."

"Wearing dresses is an old-fashioned thing; we should try to be fashionable so we don't look odd and be thought of as weird."

"Pants are more modest sometimes than some skirts."

"Pants are more comfortable for me."

"It seems to me that women who wear dresses look down on women who wear pants."

"Are we going to look down on the lost because they don't have proper attire?"

"I believe that those who preach against pants are legalistic."

See the chapter "Questions Answered on the Issue of Christian Dress" for answers to these challenges.

A Summary of the Bible's Teaching on the Christian's Dress

We have looked at many passages of Scripture and learned many lessons on the Christian's dress. Following is a summary of this issue.

1. The woman's clothing is to be modest.

This is described in the New Testament by the words "chaste," "sober," "discreet," and "shamefaced." This would forbid anything that shows the woman off in a lascivious manner or that exposes her in an indecent way.

First, modest attire covers the body properly and does not expose the parts of the body which have particular sexual appeal. The man and woman should be covered decently so that the body is not improperly displayed in a sensual manner. Isaiah 47:2 says that for a woman to bare her leg to show the thigh is nakedness. Thus immodest clothing would include short skirts, shorts, slit skirts, low blouses, short blouses that bare the midriff, deep V-necked dresses, backless dresses, halter tops, and any modern swimsuit. Immodest clothing would also include any style that uses flimsy material that can be seen through.

Second, modest attire does not sensually accent the body. Tight, clinging attire is as immodest as skimpy attire because the woman's figure is emphasized and accented, and man's attention is directed to that which is forbidden outside of marriage. The immodest clothing industry understands these things and strives to dress women seductively rather than modestly.

Third, modest attire is not extravagant. When the apostle deals with modest attire in 1 Timothy 2:9, he mentions *"broided hair, gold, pearls, and costly array."* The goal of this world's godless fashion industry is to create a haughty, ostentatious, worldly-wise look, as well as a sexual look. The godly woman will reject such fashion and clothe herself and her daughters in "modest apparel."

2. The Christian's clothing is to be sexually distinctive (Gen. 1:27; Deut. 22:5; 1 Cor. 11:14-15).

The woman's dress is to be distinctively feminine and the man's distinctively masculine. The modern unisex movement is in rebellion against Almighty God and His Word, and the Christian should have nothing whatsoever to do with any fashion associated with it.

3. The Christian's clothing is to be identified with holiness and godliness and not to be identified with anything that is evil (1 Thess. 5:22; Eph. 5:11).

If a clothing style is identified with rebellion against God's laws, with anarchy, with sexual freedom, with blasphemy, with idolatry, with moral decadence, or with any other evil it should not be worn by a Christian. This would prohibit fashions, for example, that have come out of the world of punk and rap, such as long hair on men, tight masculine jeans on women, torn jeans, low slung baggy jeans, and such. This would also prohibit tattoos with their identification with rebellion and paganism.

4. The Christian's clothing is to be characterized by separation from the world (Rom. 12:2; 2 Cor. 6:14-17; Titus 2:12-13; 1 John 2:15-16; James 4:4).

The Christian's clothing is not to be conformed to anything in the world that is associated with the lust of the flesh, the lust of the eyes, and the pride of life. Examples of fashions that are worldly are indecent female dress styles that flaunt her sexuality and ostentatious fashions that cry, "Look at me."

5. The Christian's clothing is to mark him or her as peculiar unto the Lord, as one who has been redeemed from all iniquity and who is zealous for good works (Titus 2:14).

God's people are to be separate, peculiar, different, set apart. We must bear His stamp. We must stand out from the crowd because we are walking by heaven's light. We must not fly the world's flag. When God's people are no longer peculiar before the world they have compromised the Word of God. We must fear God more than man. We must be more concerned about pleasing God than people. We must not draw back from bearing Christ's reproach in this wicked world. He said, "Whosoever therefore shall be ashamed of me and of my words in this adulterous and sinful generation; of him also shall the Son of man be ashamed, when he cometh in the glory of his Father with the holy angels" (Mk. 8:38). Paul said that if we deny Christ, he also will deny us (2 Tim. 2:12).

Pushing the Edge on Dress Standards: Borderline Modesty vs. True Modesty

In my preaching conferences I have had occasions, sadly, to observe that though a church or Christian school might have pretty good dress standards (written or unwritten) for workers and youth, many of the girls and young women dress immodestly.

I am not the only one to notice this. One pastor wrote as follows:

> "In 2006, I visited the campus of --------- Christian College and attended a chapel service. I was grieved as I watched the students assemble. Many of the girls were wearing tight, form fitting blouses and skirts. There were a lot of skirts above the knee as well as slits that went above the knee. One pastor friend refers to the slit skirt as 'peek-a-boo' skirts. How can the young men possibly keep their minds pure as they train for the ministry when so many of the girls are dressing like strange women all around them?"

Another man wrote:

> "Our church teaches and preaches separation. Our pastor has even compiled a small booklet on modest dress. Having said all that, we have had and still do have problems. In order to be a choir member or teach Sunday School, etc., we must sign a form saying we agree to the dress standards as well as many other standards of conduct. WHAT I HAVE SEEN IS, YES THEY ARE WEARING DRESSES, BUT MANY ARE FAR FROM MODEST. ... FORM FITTING CLOTHING [IS ONE OF THE PROBLEMS]. A lady can be actually wearing a reasonably nice dress that meets the standard, at least in their mind it does, but the problem is that it is at least a size too small for her! These folks are rarely confronted because they are wearing a dress, you know! I believe we easily forget modesty and become lost in 'I'm wearing a

dress attitude.' To be honest I have seen more modest pants on many lost ladies than the 'dresses on our standard-signing church ladies.' I'm not for pants; I'm just referring to our hypocrisy! It shows either a lack of discernment on their part or a worldly desire to show off the body, maybe both."

Another man described the same problem:

"I am thankful you are writing a book about dressing modestly. It is needed in this day and time when most fundamental independent Baptist Christians think that just as long as they wear a dress that comes below the knee, it's appropriate."

A lady gave the following description of the fundamental Baptist church that she attends:

"The teenagers wear the skirts that come to the knee but when they bend over or sit down...well you know. Their tops are low cut with a v and look like they were painted on. … My husband leads the music and he said he can't even look at the people because there are so many short skirts, etc."

The problem in these situations is that while the dresses might be long enough (when the woman is standing), they are still not modest because of the way they are cut or what happens to the clothing when the woman is involved with various activities.

For one thing dresses can be cut too low. Many men who wrote to me on this subject mentioned that this is a great distraction and temptation.

But we must understand that modesty is much more than merely covering nakedness. That is only a baby step in modesty. The heart of the truly modest girl or woman is sensitive to holiness and aware of her influence in this world and seeks to be truly modest from every standpoint, caring nothing about fashion or merely "walking on the edge" of modesty.

One major problem is tight clothing. In our survey of Christian men on the issue of women's dress we found that tight clothing is at least as much of a potential problem for men as skimpy clothing. Most of the men indicated that tight skirts and tight blouses and form-fitting jeans hold a "VERY great potential" for lust.

Consider the following statements:

> "You don't even need to see skin; they provide all the curves." Another man said: "I would say the Number One problem is any garment that is form fitting, be it jeans, pants, skirt, dress, shirt, whatever. Anything that is tight, no matter how long it is, leaves nothing to the imagination, and that defeats the whole purpose of covering the skin in the first place!"

> "One thing I see in my church is tight clothing. Oh, it may very well be covering but it is revealing the shape in a woman. This can be even more tantalizing to a man."

> "The point is that it is not merely the type of clothing that can trip a man up; rather it is the amount and the level of cling to the body."

Thin clothing can also be a serious modesty issue. One man wrote: "If a woman is standing so that light can shine through her skirt, although she may be covered with a garment, it is so transparent that everything is revealed. A woman can be covered yet at the same time uncovered."

There are many other ways to be "seductive" even in "modest" clothing. God, through the prophet Isaiah, rebuked the women of that day not only because of what they wore but also *because of the countenance and because of how they carried themselves*:

> "Moreover the LORD saith, Because the daughters of Zion are haughty, and walk with stretched forth necks and wanton eyes, walking and mincing as they go, and making a tinkling with their feet" (Isaiah 3:16).

One man wrote:

"It's not just clothing that can be inappropriate -- also high heel shoes. They cause the hips to gyrate when the lady walks. The secular world told us this, so why is it in the church? Bright red nail varnish on fingernails and toenails, red lip stick, seamed stockings -- that look from the '50s and '60s. [It screams out, 'Look at ME!'] It's not always what the attire is but how it is worn and the woman herself. ... Excessive use of perfume and make up -- both designed to draw men; they should be used with wisdom. Also, flirtatious natures and wanting to be noticed by the opposite sex should be reigned in."

The battleground, of course, as we have noted many times, is the heart. If a lady is worldly in her heart, she will probably not be modest even if fully clothed and she will look for ways to push the boundaries of any clothing standards with the objective of being fashionable and perhaps showing herself off.

A pastor that operates a home for troubled young women wrote as follows, "We have had girls come from homes and churches that hold to strict dress standards, but they carry themselves like strange women in modest clothing because it's in their hearts!"

It's in their hearts! It's in their hearts! Whatever is in the heart will show itself in the dress.

When young women's clothes are form fitting and push the envelope of decency on every side, it is obvious that one of two things is happening.

First, in many cases the objective is not really to be modest before the Lord but rather simply to obey man's rules and that only as long as necessary. That is a serious issue that is reflective either of an unregenerate heart or a backslidden one. It has been said that true character is demonstrated by what we do when no one is watching.

Second, there are doubtless cases in which girls and young women simply don't understand how immodest they really are in the eyes of men. They are naively going along with the current fashion and with the crowd. If this is the case, the lady in question will be open to correction and will respond to plain preaching and teaching and private exhortation on this subject.

How can a church, then, resist the problem we have described and gain true modesty in the congregation? Following are some suggestions:

True modesty requires education. The females must not merely be given a dress code but must be taught the Bible principles of modesty carefully and urged to apply them consistently. This won't happen through a sermon or a Sunday School lesson every few years. It requires making female modesty a real emphasis in the church and developing a course of instruction that will educate the people properly and in addition to that mentioning it often in the preaching/teaching ministry of the church in a kind and patient way.

True modesty requires example. It is crucial that the wives of the pastors and teachers and deacons and the older female church members understand the issue of modesty and that they are committed to it from the heart and are applying the Bible's principles consistently rather then just going by a couple of written rules. If there is a failure here, it will be reflected throughout the congregation. If the wives of church officers push the boundaries of modesty, if they are careless about their necklines and if their dresses are too tight and if fashion is more important than modesty, the church will never win this battle. Victory has to start at the top.

True modesty requires exhortation. Teaching is not enough; exhortation is also needed. The preacher is instructed to "reprove, rebuke, exhort" (2 Tim. 4:2). This goes beyond teaching. Reproving, rebuking, and exhorting are all necessary. God's people have a sin nature that tends to backslide and go after the things of the flesh and the world, and they must be reproved and exhorted to stay in the Lord's narrow paths. This ministry of reproof is as much a necessary part of the pastor's ministry as teaching. If he neglects it he is compromising. Both the males and the females of the congregation need to hear reproof on all areas of practical Christian living, and that certainly includes modest dress and separation from the world. Pastors who leave this out of their preaching will find that many things slip in the congregation because of the lack of plain reproof.

True modesty requires consistency in the preachers' children. It is not enough for a pastor to preach modesty; his family must demonstrate it before the congregation and that includes his children. I have known of many pastors who have injured their ministry by the lack of enforcement of biblical modesty in the lives of their own wives and daughters. I recall a church in Florida where the pastor was a strong preacher and a soul winner, as well as a compassionate man and a good example to the people in many ways. But his beautiful teenage daughter dressed indecently and her poor example and her father's acquiesce in the matter helped break down the separation from the world in the youth department and many young lives were ruined by the love for the world.

True modesty requires educated, concerned men. It is necessary for Christian men to understand the issues of female modesty and to take a stand for it in their homes and to support it in the church. If the women are trying to be modest but the men are worldly, the men will put pressure on the women to be more "fashionable" and "less dowdy." (And I must emphasize here that I don't think Christian women should be "dowdy." The right choice isn't between immodesty and dowdiness. It is between immodesty and modest but attractive femininity.)

True modesty requires a wise dress code. I believe strongly in dress codes for Christian workers in this day and age, but the dress code must be thorough. It is not enough to say that the women must wear dresses rather than pants. It should describe all of the important features of a modest dress, that the neck line must not be low, that the clothing must not be tight, that it must be low enough so that the leg is covered properly down below the thigh, that it must not be clingy, that it must not be sheer, etc. The issue needs to be spelled out plainly. The dress standard is not only a code; it is a teaching tool to educate the people on this matter. And dress standards for church leaders and workers is a model for for the rest of the church to follow.

Of course, if a girl or woman is worldly in her heart she will still look for ways to push the boundaries of the standards regardless of how clear they are, but that is a separate problem altogether.

Plain Clothing

Some independent Baptists and fundamentalists in general seem to be reacting to the worldliness of many churches by adopting a "plain clothes" style that is akin to the old Mennonite fashion. I can understand the rejection of worldliness, but I question the plain clothes position and fear for its end result. We should not establish doctrine and practice on the basis of "reactionism," but upon solid Bible teaching.

I know of dozens of families and churches in five states that are moving in this direction.

The Charity Fellowship (which I have written about elsewhere) has had considerable influence in popularizing the plain clothes position among some independent Baptists.

Following are some comments I would like to make about the "plain clothes" position:

1. I believe in liberty.

The believer is free to dress as he or she pleases before the Lord within the bounds of biblical modesty. When Romans 14:4 says, "Who art thou that judgest another man's servant?" it is talking about judging others on the basis of the Bible's silence. When the Bible is silent on a matter, there is personal liberty before God, and to make laws that go beyond Scripture is legalism. This is obvious from the context. Paul used the example of diet to illustrate his principle (Romans 14:2-3). There is no divinely-ordained New Testament diet, so this is a matter of liberty.

Immodest and unisex styles of clothing aside, there is individual liberty in dress. As far as I am concerned, you can wear a 1930s B.C. Ur of the Chaldees pleated robe or a 1930s A.D. Zoot suit!

Please understand that nothing I intend to say here is with the objective of taking away your freedom in Christ or discouraging earnest people who are seeking to please God. If you want to dress in some kind of plain uniform, that is your business at the end of the day.

You say, "It is my choice; I don't make it a law for others." Well and good. I'm not here to condemn godly people who want to do right before the Lord, but I would challenge you to examine why you have chosen a particular style and its possible repercussions.

2. I believe in modest dress.

Our book *Dressing for the Lord* goes into the subject of modest dress in considerable detail. The Bible definitely has something to say about how we are to dress in this sin-cursed world. Dress is not a "non issue" or a "non-essential." Dress is a language. Men look on the outward appearance and are affected by the outward appearance. The giving up of modest and godly standards of dress is one of the signs of end-times apostasy and is a large step toward the emerging church.

In this chapter on plain clothing we are not dealing with immodest or ungodly styles of dress, but I wanted to remind my readers of my position on these things so there will not be any confusion.

3. Woman is the glory of man

The Bible says the woman is the glory of the man and her hair is given for her glory (1 Cor. 11:7, 15). There is nothing wrong, then, with the woman fixing herself up in an attractive way as long as she is modest.

The prudent woman of Proverbs 31 didn't dress plainly. She weaved wool and flax and clothed her household in scarlet (Prov. 31:13, 19, 21).

The word "modest" in 1 Timothy 1:9-10 means "restrained by a sense of propriety, not bold or forward, not loose, not lewd ... not presumptuous or arrogant ... chaste, pure" (Webster 1828). It refers to discretion and moderation. When Paul says, "not with broided hair, or gold, or pearls, or costly array," it does not mean that the Christian woman can't fix her hair or wear jewelry or make up of any sort. This is a doctrine that has been forced upon the passage and it puts people into a legalistic bondage. It means, rather, that this must not be the woman's emphasis and it should not be done in worldly excess. The external appearance and fashion should not be what characterizes her. She should be characterized, rather, by "shamefacedness and sobriety and good works" (1 Tim. 2:9-10). Paul is talking about moderation.

This is clear when we compare Scripture with Scripture. Consider 1 Peter 3:3-5:

"Whose adorning let it not be that outward adorning of plaiting the hair, and of wearing of gold, or of putting on of apparel; but let it be the hidden man of the heart, in that which is not corruptible, even the ornament of a meek and quiet spirit, which is in the sight of God of great price. Whose adorning let it not be that outward adorning of plaiting the hair, and of wearing of gold, or of putting on of apparel; but let it be the hidden man of the heart, in that which is not corruptible, even the ornament of a meek and quiet spirit, which is in the sight of God of great price."

If this passage is pushed to extreme literalism, it would say that the woman should not put on apparel, which is ridiculous. Ever since man sinned in the Garden of Eden, it has been God's will that the man and woman be clothed. In reality, Peter is saying the same thing as Paul, that the woman's focus should not be on adorning her hair and wearing jewelry and following the latest fashion, but her focus should be on developing an attitude of godly submission to authority and "the ornament of a meek and quiet spirit."

Again, it is a matter of moderation as opposed to ostentatiousness. For a woman to fix up her hair within moderation and to wear some type of modest jewelry and makeup and such is not wrong. It becomes wrong when it ceases to be moderate and modest, when it detracts from godliness. Her external appearance should reflect and adorn her inner character rather than contradict it.

It is obvious that there is a lot of personal liberty in the context of this biblical principle.

4. We must not strain at gnats and swallow camels

Jesus charged the Pharisees with straining at gnats and swallowing camels (Matthew 23:23-24), because they focused on things of lesser importance to the destruction of the most important. They majored on the minors. There are two great lessons here. First, Jesus taught that everything in Scripture has some importance (contrary to the popular "in non-essentials liberty" doctrine), but He also taught that everything is not of equal importance and should not receive our equal attention.

A correct interpretation of 1 Timothy 2 and 1 Peter 3 helps us avoid the carnal attitude of judging every little perceived infraction of apparel. I am reminded of a family that left a good independent Baptist church because they disagreed with how that some women in the church wore slight heels and the pastor wouldn't restrict them from singing in the choir on that basis. Some can't countenance any makeup or any jewelry whatsoever. They are so focused on this type of thing that they can't minister properly to those with spiritual needs.

They are straining at gnats and swallowing camels.

Once you start down that road, where does it end? Typically it results in a critical spirit whereby instead of seeking to help people, the individual judges them and tries to stay away from them.

5. The Great Commission will result in churches that are deeply imperfect.

A Scriptural church that is focused on fulfilling Christ's Great Commission (Matthew 28:18-20; Mark 16:15; Acts 1:8) will be deeply imperfect, because it will be populated by new believers who still carry lots of worldly baggage and by people representing broken homes and such who in this life will never achieve a level of ideal Christianity and family life.

When brethren of the previously described mindset come together in an attempt to form a perfectly separated church built around a strong family emphasis, they are in danger of forming an inward-looking cult. Those in society with deeply defective families (meaning the vast majority today); those who are divorced or living together out of wedlock and are in a spiritual and moral mess; those who are single, etc., don't feel comfortable enough around them to be helped. But these are the very types that Jesus sought out and ministered to.

We have been church planters since 1979, and the church we are working with currently is eight years old. Practically all of the members were won to Christ out of Hinduism and the world in general as opposed to coming from other churches. Most of the members are either divorced or on their second or third marriages or married to unbelievers or single. Several of the women are married to unbelievers, and they are mistreated, some even beaten. Every week in our main service we have a representation of female visitors who dress immodestly and wear idolatrous tikkas and male visitors with ponytails and earrings and such and who are idolators and fornicators and drunkards and liars and thieves. Of course, our objective is to see them saved and sanctified, but it doesn't happen overnight.

This is what you find in churches that are reaching the community with the gospel. It's messy business!

6. The principle of being all things to all men

Along this same line, I believe the adoption of Mennonite-like "plain style" uniforms can infringe on the Pauline principle of being all things to all men.

"Give none offence, neither to the Jews, nor to the Gentiles, nor to the church of God: Even as I please all men in all things, not seeking mine own profit, but the profit of many, that they may be saved" (1 Corinthians 10:32, 33).

Paul didn't want to offend people for no good reason, because his objective was to win them to Christ.

Looking back, I don't think someone who dressed like the Amish could have won me to Christ. It appears too cultish, too strange. I wouldn't have listened to them.

By all means, I am not advocating dressing in worldly fashions in order to fit in the world. That is unscriptural. The child of God has no liberty to disobey Scripture for any objective whatsoever, regardless of how noble. Thus, a believer has no liberty to dress in unisex or immodest fashions.

What I am saying is that Paul's principle tells me that we should dress in a manner that allows us to "fit in" with society as much as biblically possible in order to communicate the gospel most effectively.

We are called peculiar people in Scripture, but that doesn't have the modern meaning of odd; it means that we are God's exclusive possession because we have been purchased by Christ. The Greek word translated "peculiar" in 1 Peter 2:9 is translated "possession" in Ephesians 1:14 and "purchased" in Acts 20:28.

The child of God shouldn't be odd for odd's sake, because he has a higher calling than merely to dress as he pleases.

We should be separated from unbelieving society by our godliness rather than by living in communes and wearing eccentric dress.

I realize that for a woman to dress modestly and godly in this present world will mean that she will stand out. For a woman to wear a modest dress today instead of pants will guarantee that she stands out from the crowd, but an attractive, modest dress is one thing, whereas a plain style costume is another.

7. The danger of tradition becoming law

How did the Amish get to where they are today? I am referring to those who ride around in horse-drawn buggies, refuse to use electricity, and dress alike in uniforms. How did they become living museum showpieces?   How did they become the epitome of Pharisaical legalism? Their lifestyle can't be defended from Scripture. It's ridiculous, actually. How did it happen?

I will tell you how it happened. It happened *gradually* over generations as tradition became law.

At first some of them wore suspenders and black hats as a matter of choice and personal liberty, but eventually this settled into a law whereby everyone had to conform to the same vain tradition. Those who joined them had to give up personal liberty and were required to submit to the group tradition.

It happened originally through a desire to be separated from the evil of this present world system, but they gradually turned sound biblical separation into cultish isolationism. The Amish today, typically, don't win people to Christ, and if they do they turn their converts into the same type of legalists and isolationists that they have become.

I will conclude where I started. We must not establish doctrine and practice on the basis of "reactionism" (reacting to the worldliness of typical churches), but upon solid Bible teaching and principles. We must flee from legalism as from a dangerous snake. I am referring to exalting human tradition to the authority of divine law, as the Pharisees did.

Questions Answered on the Issue of Christian Dress

I have been writing on the subject of the Christian's dress for decades, and the following are answers to questions and challenges I have received on this issue from readers. In many cases people completely misunderstand and misrepresent this issue, and I appreciate this opportunity to correct the record from my perspective.

WHY DO YOU FOCUS MORE ON WOMEN'S CLOTHING THAN ON MEN'S?

We focus on women's clothing because that is what the Bible focuses on. When Jesus warned about the look of adulterous lust, he addressed the men as being guilty of that rather than the women. "But I say unto you, That whosoever looketh on a woman to lust after her hath committed adultery with her already in his heart" (Mat. 5:28). I don't know of any passage in Scripture that addresses such an exhortation to women. Further, the two major New Testament passages on modest dress (1 Timothy 2:9-10; 1 Peter 3:1-4) are addressed to women rather than to men.

The reason for this is that the man is more inclined to lust through the eye-gate than the woman because of the way he was created. The woman is not nearly as visual in her sexuality as the man.

In the book *For Women Only: What You Need to Know about the Inner Lives of Men,* author Shaunti Feldhahn describes a time when her husband Jeff told her that he didn't understand why she was so amazed at her findings about how visual a man's sexuality is. It turned out that he was equally amazed at how un-visual her sexuality is. Following is the conversation they had:

Jeff: "But you knew men were visual, right?"

Shaunti: "Well, yes, of course. But since most women aren't, I just didn't get it. I just don't experience things the same way you do."

Jeff: "Maybe we just use different language to describe it. For example, think of a movie star that you find physically attractive--Tom Cruise, say. After we've seen one of his movies, how many times will that attractive image rise up in your mind the next day?"

Shaunti: "Never."

Jeff: "I must not be explaining myself correctly. I mean, how many times will a thought of what he looked like with his shirt off just sort of pop up in your head?"

Shaunti: "Never."

Jeff: "Never--as in *never*?"

Shaunti: "Zero times. It just doesn't happen."

Jeff: "(After a long pause) "Wow."

She concludes the story this way:

> "That was the end of that conversation, but it wasn't the end of the issue. When my husband recently told this story to our home group, he confessed that at first he thought I was embarrassed to admit that I really might have pictures of Tom Cruise in my head! It wasn't until he watched me tell the story to a group of women, and watched most of the women say 'never' right along with me, that the lightning bold hit. Our little exchange did more to teach Jeff and me how each of us is wired--and not wired--than almost anything else. And I hope my new understanding is helping me be more supportive and protective of my husband in today's culture" (*For Women Only*, pp. 116, 117, 118).

My own wife confirmed this to me. When I talked with her about how she is affected by men who wear tight spandex shorts or go shirt-less, she said it is not a matter of lust. It is a matter, rather, of disrespect. She said she loses respect for such a man. She said that if she sees a well-built man going without a shirt or in a small "muscle flex" underwear-type shirt, her thought is simply that he is showing off.

Thus I conclude that what men wear is important, but it is not so much a matter of helping the women not to lust sexually as a matter of maintaining their respect. The Christian man should not run around in a skimpy undershirt or shirt-less, so that he can be a proper representative of Christ in this needy world and not run the potential of someone thinking that he is careless and disrespectable.

SINCE GOD LOOKS ON THE HEART, WHY ARE YOU CONCERNED ABOUT APPEARANCE?

It is true that God looks on the heart, but the same passage of Scripture also reminds us that man looks on the outward appearance. The Scripture in question is 1 Samuel 16:7.

> "But the LORD said unto Samuel, Look not on his countenance, or on the height of his stature; because I have refused him: for the LORD seeth not as man seeth; for man looketh on the outward appearance, but the LORD looketh on the heart" (1 Sam. 16:7).

The context for this passage was the ordination of a new king in Israel to replace Saul. The prophet Samuel was instructed to go to the household of Jesse to choose a king from among Jesse's sons. When Samuel considered the young men, he was immediately impressed with Eliab because of his stature, and that is when God instructed him not to look on the outward appearance because "the Lord looketh on the heart."

This does not mean that the outward appearance is of no importance and that God has no interest in how a Christian dresses. In fact, this verse has nothing whatsoever to do with clothing. Samuel was not impressed by Eliab's clothing but by his physical stature. The fact that God looks on the heart does not negate the verses in Scripture that deal with modest apparel.

Further, this verse plainly states that man does look on the outward appearance. This is reason enough to be careful about how we dress. Man judges the book by its cover. Since our dress is a language, we must be careful that we are preaching the right message by how we are clothed.

A person can be right in his external appearance and not be right with God in his heart, but when a person is right with God internally he or she will be concerned about dressing correctly and not causing others to stumble.

MEN ARE GOING TO SIN ANYWAY, SO WHAT IS THE BIG DEAL?

One individual wrote to say:

> "In my years of talking with other men, I have concluded that each of us find different things appealing and different things as a 'turn off,' for lack of a better term. Yes, I know that women can dress seductively and 'draw' the attention of men but you can dress the entire population of women in burkas and men will still lust. Lust is more from the heart than in what women wear. Women by their very nature attract men."

The answer to this challenge is as follows. Though worldly men might lust even when women are dressed modestly, because lust is first of all a matter of the imagination of the heart, this does not mean that it doesn't matter how women dress. The man who wrote the above challenge admits that women can dress seductively and draw the attention of men sexually because that is a powerful temptation to men. Thus, by his own testimony, it is obvious that a Christian woman has a responsibility to do whatever she can to reduce this temptation.

Further, I am convinced that men do not have nearly the problem with lust when women are dressed modestly as when they are dressed seductively. A man who wants to entertain his carnal nature does not meditate upon a modestly dressed godly woman. When men want to lust and entertain their carnal nature, they find a way to look at women either entirely naked or dressed seductively or they merely think about women in this way, so that their imagination can be excited.

I know personally that when women dress in a truly feminine and modest manner it is a great help to me spiritually and morally, and the vast majority of the men who have written to me on this issue have said the same thing. There have been times when I was traveling and have seen a group of girls and women dressed in a truly modest manner that I have gone over to them and thanked them for this.

I am convinced that dress and character and actions are intimately associated. When American women commonly dressed in a feminine and much more modest manner than they do today, the nation was MUCH more righteous. When women dressed modestly there was MUCH less rape, divorce, homosexuality, murder, adultery, child delinquency, drug abuse, you name it.

The late Gordon Sears, a godly Bible evangelist and musician, observed:

> "When the standard of dress is lowered, then the standard of conduct is also lowered. When the standard of conduct is lowered, then the sense of value in God's truth is lowered."

Any argument against trying to maintain godly dress standards in Bible-believing churches ignores these important truths.

WHY DON'T YOU JUST FOLLOW THE EXAMPLE OF THE MUSLIMS AND HAVE THE WOMEN WEAR BURKAS?

Our objective with teaching biblical modesty is entirely different from that of a Muslim society that requires the burka. (A burka -- also spelled *burqa* or *burkha* -- in its most extreme incarnation is a robe-like gown that covers the woman entirely, from the top of her head to the floor, with veiled holes for the eyes. In its more conservative mode it is the same sack-like covering from the top of the neck to the floor accompanied by a hood-like head covering that leaves only the woman's face showing. There are several variations. The burka is worn over the woman's ordinary clothing when she is in public and is taken off in the home.)

The burka in Muslim nations doesn't produce godliness in the society for the simple reason that the burka is not really about modesty in a biblical sense. Yes, the burka covers the woman entirely, but the message the burka speaks is that women are property, that the woman is nothing in herself without the man, that women belong to men in an exclusive sense going far beyond and contrary to what the Bible teaches. The wide-spread practice of female castration in Muslim societies demonstrates my point, as does the law that a woman who is raped is punished as an adulteress unless she has multiple witnesses to support her charge. The woman is only a "thing" to be treated or mistreated as men see fit.

I agree with the following description of the message of the burka:

> "The top-to-toe burka, with its sinister, airless little grille, is more than an instrument of persecution, it is a public tarring and feathering of female sexuality. It transforms any woman into an object of defilement too untouchably disgusting to be seen. ... In its objectifying of women, it turns them into cowering creatures demanding and expecting violence and victimization. ... More moderate versions of the garb -- the dull, uniform coat to the ground and the plain headscarf -- have much the same effect" ("Behind the Burka," *The Guardian*, London, Sept. 28, 2001).

A godly biblical standard of modesty, on the other hand, does not degrade women. Rather it exalts women as valuable and respectable and important and desirable, not merely for sex or for the labor she can perform and not merely as piece of property, but because she is a special divine creation made in God's image and made for a very important purpose in this world and made to honor and cherish in a godly sense, not merely by one man in the bond of matrimony but by society at large.

A truly feminine and godly manner of dress causes men to look upon women in this biblical fashion. Many women have told me that they are treated with a great deal more respect out in the public when they dress modestly.

SHOULDN'T WE JUST TEACH THE BIBLE AND LET THE HOLY SPIRIT DEAL WITH THIS ISSUE?

One man wrote to say:

> "I have found that the closer people truly get to the Lord through the proper TEACHING of the Word, the more clothes they wear. Not sermons, seminars, or books on clothing but just getting the Word in them. Verse by verse."

I agree 100% with the importance of careful and systematic preaching and teaching of God's Word. Christian living that is not based on such a foundation can be very shallow and inconsistent and hypocritical.

But I would never try to contrast systematic teaching with topical teaching or imply that one is not important, because the fact is that *both* are important. It is very useful and powerful to preach on issues of practical Christian living by bringing together Bible passages dealing with a certain subject and focusing the believer's attention on that particular subject and helping him grasp a thorough understanding of it. It is same with teaching Bible doctrine. A well-rounded course of Bible instruction includes comprehensive, systematic, expository teaching as well as topical teaching, and it is the Holy Spirit who leads the preacher in his selection of a particular method at any given time.

Further, I have heard from many women who have told me that the issue of modesty didn't get down to the practical level with them until some preacher made it a focus in a series of sermons or lessons. Women told me that it wasn't enough to see the godly example of the older women in the Lord, even ones that they highly respected, but it was necessary to hear it taught and to hear it taught from men.

One woman wrote:

> "My husband became a pastor and he believed in teaching the whole counsel of God -- which included modest apparel for women. ALTHOUGH I HAD BEEN TAUGHT THE SAME THING [from women] IT DIDN'T REALLY HIT HOME UNTIL I HEARD A MAN TEACH ON IT. I listened to my husband preach the Word of God and I gained understanding. It wasn't long before I came to understand more completely God's design for women and how He wants them to present themselves. I now have a Biblical conviction, thanks to a preacher who was doing his job. ... Basically I did not come to have a Biblical conviction until I clearly saw it from God's Word. TODAY THIS SUBJECT IS NOT OFTEN PREACHED FROM THE PULPIT. THE PASTOR SAYS, 'I'LL LEAVE IT TO MY WIFE TO TEACH THE LADIES.' THE WIFE SAYS, 'I'LL JUST LIVE THE RIGHT WAY AND TEACH BY MY EXAMPLE.' IT DOESN'T WORK. IT DIDN'T WORK FOR ME AND SADLY IT ISN'T WORKING FOR THE MAJORITY OF YOUNG CHRISTIAN WOMEN IN CHURCHES TODAY."

This is a loud challenge to those fundamental Baptist preachers who don't want to deal with this issue plainly from the pulpit.

The 200 e-mails I have received just recently on this subject from men and women in many parts of the world bear out what this lady is saying. There are many churches that have a godly pastor's wife and some other women who are setting the example and even have some written dress standards, but the matter of truly modest dress isn't "trickling" down to the girls and the younger women. A couple of pastors wrote to say that they do not believe this is a matter for the pulpit. I could not disagree more. It is, in fact, a matter that needs to be dealt with in a church from every direction in a kind and godly and patient and humble manner.

As for expository preaching being sufficient in itself to train the people in modesty with no need for a topical approach, if that were true it would be born out on every hand. There are many evangelical and fundamentalist wanna-be evangelical churches that feature expository preaching and teaching, but in many cases today this book-by-book, chapter-by-chapter, verse-by-verse ministry does not produce a congregation of girls and women that dress modestly.

WHY CAN'T THE MEN JUST KEEP THEIR EYES TO THEMSELVES?

We have answered this under the chapter "Isn't This Basically the Man's Problem?"

I BELIEVE DRESS STANDARDS JUST PRODUCE PRIDE AND HYPOCRISY

One man wrote:

> "I have been around a bunch of women who are not modest, but prudish, putting people down who aren't quite to their level spiritually, just to make their own empty lives feel better. When a preacher or members of a congregation beat a new Christian into submission by changing their outward appearance, God is deprived of the chance of changing their heart. They learn only to judge their walk by the approval of others and stop listening to the leading of the Holy Spirit."

I have heard this type of sentiment many times, and I am sad to say that there probably are churches that fit this description. I can say unequivocally, though, that we do not support anything like this and have always striven to maintain dress standards in an environment of humble heart-level obedience to Christ. I do not recommend churches that fit the previous description.

If a group of Christian women do fit this description, they have a spiritual problem and need to repent and the church in question needs to figure out what it is doing wrong; but such a problem, even if it were extensive, does not discredit the necessity of maintaining biblical standards of modest apparel. Many people have justified their lack of attendance to church with the charge that there are hypocrites there, but the fact that some people live the Christian life hypocritically does not discredit true godly Christian living, it only highlights the urgency of the true item.

We also do not approve of churches "beating a new Christian into submission" in the matter of dress. There doubtless is such a thing but it is wrong.

Many times, though, that which is called "beating into submission" is simply a sincere and godly zeal for holiness. Who will say that it is wrong to teach new converts the whole counsel of God? Who will say that it is wrong for mature saints to teach immature saints how to live holy lives? Who will say that it is wrong for the pastor to preach on any subject found in Scripture, whether or not new converts are present? Who will say that it is wrong for the older women to teach the younger women to be chaste as Titus demands, and where does the Bible say that new converts are exempt from this ministry or that the older women's teaching on chasteness cannot be applied to dress?

The thing that is also necessary in this context is humility, patience, and compassion. I recently met a man who had been a member of an independent Baptist church for three years and he still had a pony tail that hung down to his waist. During those three years, preachers had preached against long hair on men from the pulpit and his own wife had told him that it is wrong, even though she is the one who had encouraged him to grow it before they were converted, and his own pastor had talked to him about it. He resisted for three years before he cut it, and had remained a faithful member of the church, because the pastor genuinely loved him and the people were patient with him. (Part of that time he kept it hidden under his shirt.) When I talked to him about it and observed that many individuals would have left and gone to another church under those circumstances, he said, "I'm not going anywhere; this is where God has blessed me." That's the way it should be. The church that I first joined had the same attitude. It was very fundamentalist and was strict about Christian living and the teaching and example of the older members was excellent, but no one tried to ram things down my throat, so to speak; they loved me and were patient with me about my long hair, rock & roll, smoking, etc.

This is the way it should be.

At the same time, a church has every right to preach and teach plainly on any subject in God's Word and also to set standards for workers and for those who represent it in any area of ministry, because the congregation and community judge the church by those who assume such positions. Though it might be O.K. for a man be a member of the church for three years even though he wears a pony tail tucked under his shirt, such a man should not be an usher, let alone a deacon; and though a woman might be a member of the church even if she wears a mini-skirt for awhile after her conversion, she should never teach a Sunday School class in that immature and immodest condition. (Of course, at some point, church members should be expected to grow up!)

As for Christians learning to dress a certain way just to please people rather than learning to follow the Holy Spirit, the churches should always aim to discourage that. It is natural, of course, for young Christians sometimes to have their eyes more on people than on Christ, just as a toddler looks to his parents for guidance. But a godly preacher's desire and objective is not to make the people dependent on him for their standards of Christian living. It is to build them up in Christ and in His Word so that they can stand on their own feet. A godly preacher has the same objective as godly mother and father who want to train the children in such a manner that they are no longer dependent upon their parents.

IT IS NO ONE ELSE'S BUSINESS WHAT I WEAR.

The Bible says, "For none of us liveth to himself, and no man dieth to himself" (Romans 14:7).

If I am saved I have been purchased by the Lord Jesus Christ and I am His bondservant. "For ye are bought with a price: therefore glorify God in your body, and in your spirit, which are God's" (1 Corinthians 6:20).

The Lord Jesus and His apostles left us the example of dying to self and living for others. Christ said, "For I came down from heaven, not to do mine own will, but the will of him that sent me" (John 6:38). Paul said, "Even as I please all men in all things, not seeking mine own profit, but the profit of many, that they may be saved" (1 Cor. 10:33).

IF I REQUIRE MODEST DRESS FOR MY DAUGHTERS THEY WILL REBEL.

I heard of one lady who said that she allows her daughters to dress in a worldly way because, "You have to let them pick their own style or they will grow up to hate the Lord and have nothing to do with church."

My answer to this is that the parents must not only require modesty from their children, they must also teach them to understand these issues and must win them to Christ and reach their hearts so they will want to continue in the right paths.

Christian parents that allow their sons or daughters to dress in a worldly fashion so as not to lose them to the world HAVE ALREADY LOST THEM TO THE WORLD!

If your daughters are already teenagers and are rebelling and dressing immodestly, you have a serious problem, because the best time to win them to modesty is when they are younger. It is much more difficult when they are teens. By God's grace it might be done, but suggestions along those lines are beyond the bounds of this book.

I realize that some Christians find themselves in difficult situations over which they have little control and in such cases their options are limited. You might be married, for example, to an unsaved or carnal individual who does not support modest standards of dress and, in fact, tries to undermine your efforts in this matter. You might be divorced and required by law to share custody of your children with an unsaved or carnal former spouse who is antagonistic to your faith and is intent on undermining your fundamentalist Christian influence with the children. In such a case, you must do the best you can with what options you have and trust the Lord to make something good come out of a bad situation that is usually the result of sin and unwise decisions in the past. The Lord is good and compassionate and powerful, and we can trust Him with full confidence in any situation. "Say not thou, I will recompense evil; but wait on the LORD, and he shall save thee" (Proverbs 20:22).

AS AN OLDER WOMAN I DON'T THINK THE MODESTY ISSUE IS VERY SIGNIFICANT IN MY CASE; MEN AREN'T GOING TO LUST AFTER ME. THIS IS AN ISSUE FOR YOUNGER WOMEN.

Modest dress is an issue both for older and younger women because the older are to be examples to and teachers of the younger (Titus 2:3-5). If the older women let down their standards for the sake of comfort or carelessness, the younger women will be negatively affected and the cause of

Christ blasphemed. The older woman needs to ask herself, "What type of example am I to the younger women and to my grandchildren?"

Further, a reader of the first edition of this book made a good point when he said: "Older women need to know that they can cause lust in a man's heart too. Some would ask, 'Who would lust after a 65-year-old woman?' Well, a 65-year-old man would." I recall a saying I read in *Reader's Digest* years ago. A man said, "I am at the age that when I go to a wedding the mother of the bride is more interesting to me than the bride."

GOD IS IN THE BUSINESS OF CHANGING HEARTS AND MINDS, AND THAT IS MORE IMPORTANT THAN PREACHING ON DRESS.

God is definitely in the business of changing hearts and minds, and the heart is the real battleground in the matter of dress. That's where we started in this book and that's what we have emphasized throughout. If the heart is not reached and a girl or woman wears a certain style of clothing for the wrong motive, the battle is not yet won. We know that a person can wear the right clothing and have a carnal heart.

The heart being the battle ground also reminds us that it is not enough to set forth dress standards. Oftentimes when I have preached in churches, especially those that have Christian schools, I have observed that even though the young women dressed according to the standards and were basically covered up, they were not modest. Their clothes were form fitting and pushed the envelope on every side. It was obvious that the heart was not in it.

At the same time, the fact that the heart is the battleground and the focus does not mean that the physical realm is of no importance. The Bible says the believer is to glorify God both in spirit and in body (1 Cor. 6:20). Since God clothed the first man and woman after they sinned and has given standards for dress in the Scriptures, it is obvious that this is not something that is to be ignored by the churches.

Further, it is the preaching and teaching of God's Word that changes hearts and minds! That's what I am in the ministry for. The name for my publishing ministry is based on this fact. "For the commandment is a lamp; and the law is light; and reproofs of instruction are the way of life" (Proverbs 6:23).

PEOPLE DON'T GO TO CHURCH TO BE TOLD THEY ARE NOT DRESSING RIGHT. THEY GO TO CHURCH TO LEARN ALL ABOUT AN ALMIGHTY SAVIOR AND THE CARE AND COMFORT HE GIVES.

Let me say to this argument, first of all, that I do not believe a church should try to set dress standards for visitors. When people come to church as visitors they should be treated with understanding and patience. In many cases they are unsaved, and the thing the unsaved person needs to hear is not dress standards but the Gospel of Jesus Christ.

Churches need to be patient and of tender mercy even with true believers who attend but who do not yet conform to the Bible's standards for Christian living. We need to give them time to grow, to be taught, and to have an opportunity to respond to God's Word. As I have mentioned, I'm glad that when I first started attending a fundamental Baptist church in 1973 as a brand new Christian they did not say anything about my shoulder-length hair or my smoking habit or my tendency to attend Hollywood movie theaters or my love for rock & roll or the fact that I still spent time with my old reprobate buddies. They were so kind and patient with me, and for that I thank the Lord. I believe that is a godly way of treating such cases. God dealt with me through the example of the church members and through the preaching and teaching of His Word and the conviction of the Holy Spirit and gradually I put away those worldly ways.

At the same time, I believe a church has both the right and the responsibility to set specific dress standards for leaders and workers and for anyone who represents the church before the congregation and the community, including those who sing in the choir or take up the offerings or help in the nursery or whatever. In fact, one of the best ways that a church can maintain modest dress standards is to require it of all workers. This sets an excellent example for the entire church, including visitors and new converts. Such standards also set a high moral goal for Christians to aspire to. I remember as a young Christian that I was motivated to quit smoking, at least in part, because I knew that it was not allowed in the Bible School that I wanted to attend. The standard helped motivate me to do right in Christian living.

Secondly, the preacher's job is not only to preach about the love and comfort of Jesus Christ but also to preach His holiness and righteous demands for Christian living. The preacher's job is to preach the whole counsel of God (Acts 20:27), and this includes those things on separation from the world and modest dress and dying to self and glorifying Christ in all things. The preacher who fails to do this and focuses instead on the "positive," compromises his divine obligation to preach the whole Word of God, to "reprove, rebuke, exhort" (2 Timothy 4:2), to "speak, and exhort, and rebuke with all authority" (Titus 2:15). The Word of God must not only be taught; it must be preached!

I AM NOT PERSONALLY CONVICTED ABOUT DRESSING AFTER THE STANDARDS YOU HAVE DESCRIBED.

The main way that God guides His people is through the Scriptures. *Feelings and "convictions" are very undependable.* The heart is "deceitful above all things" (Jer. 17:9). We can deceive ourselves about our real motives. The Scripture gives some very clear teaching on the issue of modesty. We are to cover our nakedness from our chests to our thighs. We are to not conform to the world's patterns. We are to avoid dressing in a fashion that is seductive to men. We are to avoid breaking down the divine walls of separation between the male and the female. The woman is to dress in a modest and shamefaced manner. Those are clear scriptural teachings and they are true regardless of how I might feel about it.

Multitudes of people are convinced that they are following God's will even though they are living in disobedience to clear Scripture. Many women have written to tell me that they are sure God has called them to preach to men and/or pastor churches. People who have written to tell me that they are convinced that God has led them to be a Seventh-day Adventist or a Roman Catholic. Mormons talk about a "burning in the breast" that convinces them to follow Mormonism. There are homosexuals who are convinced that God is blessing their reprobate lifestyle.

The standard for righteousness is not a feeling of conviction or a feeling of any sort; it is the Word of God. This is the lamp unto our feet and the light unto our paths (Psa. 119:105). God warns me not to lean unto my own understanding (Prov. 3:5) and not to trust in my heart (Prov. 28:26).

> "It may sound spiritual to say, 'God is not leading me to change the way I dress. As soon as I am convicted about it, I will change.' But when we look at ourselves in the mirror, and see upon our body the styles that are peculiar to the world's standards and which cannot be scripturally defended, nor in any way serve to announce Christ as Lord of our life, neither does it distinguish us from an unregenerate world, then pick up our Bible and read, 'And be not conformed to this world but be ye transformed...' (Rom. 12:2), upon what logical, biblical reasoning can we say, 'OK God, I understand what your Word says, now if you will convict me about my dress, I'll know that you really mean for me to change'? ... Relying upon a feeling of conviction as a prerequisite for obedience to what the scripture teaches is not only an evasion of

responsibility, but a reversal of divine order. OBEDIENCE IS NOT THE RESULT OF CONVICTION. CONVICTION IS THE PRODUCT OF OBEDIENCE" (David Kidd, *The Fall and Rise of Christian Standards*, pp. 66, 67).

SHOULD WOMEN ONLY WEAR DRAB SACK DRESSES?

I, for one, believe it is important for women to dress not only modestly but also pleasantly and prettily. The woman was made after the man, to adorn the man. She is most definitely his better half when it comes to appearance, and it is not wrong for a woman to look her best within the bounds of true godliness. I'm not talking about trying to be fashionable or to impress anyone. I'm not talking about "dolling up." I am talking about sweet, godly femininity and true loveliness. A modestly and nicely dressed woman is a pleasant thing for a man. He can enjoy her appearance without lusting. At least I have found that to be true, and many men have told me the same thing. If she fixes her hair and wears cosmetics discreetly and attires herself in pleasant attire, all with moderation and shamefacedness, she is only being what God made her to be, a woman.

A good answer to this was given in the book *Dress: The Heart of the Matter* by Shirley Starr and Lori Waltemyer:

> "There are two indefensible trends in this area, and both are out of balance. The first trend is to be worldly in our dress, which as we have discussed earlier is sinful and out of balance. The second trend is to be drab, dowdy, and unkempt in our appearance. This, too, is wrong and out of balance. ... Remember the Proverbs 31 Lady. She girded her loins with strength and honor through God's Word, and she clothed her family and herself with scarlet, tapestry, silk, and purple. ... Colors and pretty clothes are not wrong. God made colors and the resources to make fabric. We need not be drab and unbecoming, nor do we need to be immodest and look like ladies of the street. May

we find God's balance and apply it to our lives in the area of beauty."

ARE WE GOING TO LOOK DOWN ON THE LOST BECAUSE THEY DON'T HAVE PROPER ATTIRE? WHAT ABOUT THE POOR?

Some would ask, "Are we going to look down on the lost because they don't have proper attire? And what about the poor and those who come in with disheveled hair and tattered clothes? Should we accost them and tell them to go home and change? What if that is all they have to wear?"

This challenge, which is quoted from an e-mail I received from a Christian woman, is rather ridiculous and it shows how far some will go in their effort to discredit the teaching of modest dress standards.

We are certainly not saying that we should look down on anyone, nor are we saying that churches should have a high dress code for visitors. We want sinners to attend church so they can hear the gospel and have the opportunity to come to Christ, and we do not meet them at the door and make sure that they are dressed properly. If someone comes attired in something painfully and shockingly immodest perhaps we should try to help them find something else to wear, but for the most part dress issues are not dealt with until after the person comes to Christ. We try to do everything possible within the bounds of Scripture and reason to avoid offending the sinner so that he can have an opportunity to hear the Word of God and be saved. Many times, though, he or she gets offended in spite of our best efforts just because they are so antagonistic to biblical Christianity.

When it comes to church members and church workers, it is a different story. When someone trusts Christ and is born again he or she is bought with a price and is then to learn how to glorify God in body and spirit (1 Cor. 6:20). The church has every right to preach the whole counsel of God, including those parts about separation from the world, dying to self, and modesty. It also has every right to set dress standards for Christian workers because they represent the church and therefore the name of Christ in the community and they set the standards for the entire church by how they live and dress.

I WEAR PANTS BECAUSE THERE ARE MANY THINGS I CAN'T DO IN A MODEST MANNER IF I WEAR A DRESS.

I have heard this many times, but many godly women of past and present have dressed in a feminine fashion and have still been able to do all sorts of things, riding horses, snow skiing, plowing fields, tossing hay from a barn loft, you name it.

One woman testifies:

> "Our foremothers settled this land, built houses, planted gardens and tended animals in long skirts and beautiful dresses. Even their aprons were wonderful to behold! Surely in our day of microwaves, washing machines, and vacuum cleaners, we can do our chores with as much feminine flair as they. Personally, I feel it is uplifting to the spirit to go through each day in womanly attire. Let's dignify our work by dressing appropriately and beautifully for it!" ("Through the Week in Feminine Dress," http://www.ladiesagainstfeminism.com/articles/weekinfemininedress/mrschancey.htm).

One woman wrote to me on this issue and described how she likes dresses even in the cold and on a farm:

> "Dresses are easy for me, far more comfortable, and in the winter, extra shielding against the cold. Lest they think we need run around bare legged underneath, there are any number of leggings and warmies that go nicely, and the one or two loose flouncy skirts on the outside are that much more protection to me in freezing cold winds which we get a lot of. The skirts just cut the wind chill. I often wear the leggings all the way to the ankle covered with a

boot and no one ever sees the leggings. I have my farm dresses, wonderful, comfortable tough denim, with big pockets to carry my carrots and vitamin C (chewable) for the goats, or eggs from the chicken house or tools or screws and nails, or hoof trimming tools. Can't beat them."

One man wrote:

"My mother is 88 years old and worked in the cotton fields alongside my father back when we did it all by hand. I've never seen my mother or either of my grandmothers in pants or shorts and they all worked in the fields. I have never seen any of the women who raised me in any of the items that you mentioned. I thank God for the example they were to me."

I can say the same thing. My maternal grandmother died in 1976 when she was 80 years old and she never wore pants in her life. Neither did my paternal grandmother, who died in 1971 at age 73. One of my favorite pictures is of my maternal grandmother in a field hoeing turnip greens wearing her modest dress and her bonnet to ward off the hot Florida sun. That generation is gone, of course. My generation (I was born in 1949) is the last one for whom it was common that their grandmothers wore only dresses. *But the fact that the times have changed and Western society has corrupted itself and traded God's principles for the Devil's does not stop individual Christian women from keeping the light of modesty burning in their personal lives and passing the torch to their daughters and granddaughters.*

I believe that a good choice for some occasions is for girls and women to wear modest culottes that are cut like a loose-fitting skirt. One woman who raised nine children, five of them girls, wrote:

"Culottes are great for everyday! My girls never had to give up climbing trees, riding bikes or horses, they even played street hockey with their brothers. Bowling, volleyball, hikes, gardening, roller blading, and floor cleaning all go great with culottes!" (http://www.myculottes.com).

Another possible choice for some occasions is to wear leggings underneath a long skirt or dress.

One woman wrote to ask:

> "As a Christian woman who wants to be physically fit, I need to know what modest clothing other Christian women use for active wear, such as sports, aerobic activities, and mat exercises."

Culottes would be one possibility. In my estimation, aerobic exercise for a woman should be done in the privacy of one's own home rather than in public, anyway. And *if a sport requires any sort of immodest or unisex attire, it isn't worth it!* As one woman wrote, "If you can't do a certain activity while dressed properly, you don't need to do it!"

Jesus challenged us to *"seek ye first the kingdom of God, and his righteousness; and all these things shall be added unto you"* (Matthew 6:33). If I put God first and honor His Word, I will enjoy His provision and blessings, and there is nothing that is worth losing that over.

There is one more thing I would like to say in reply to this challenge ("I have to wear pants on some occasions to be modest"). *It is usually just a red herring, because women who throw out this challenge commonly dress in pants on any occasion.*

IN BIBLE TIMES BOTH MEN AND WOMEN WORE ROBES. JESUS WORE LONG ROBES IN HIS DAYS, AS WAS THE MANNER WITH ALL MEN, AND SO DID THE WOMEN. DID THEY CALL HIM EFFEMINATE?

In reply we will first quote the Bible itself, which makes it clear that the attire of men and women in ancient Israel was distinctively different, and that is what matters.

> "The woman shall not wear that which pertaineth unto a man, neither shall a man put on a woman's garment: for all that do so are abomination unto the LORD thy God" (Deuteronomy 22:5).

Why would the Bible say this if men and women's attire were not clearly distinguishable in that place and time?

Further, men wore breeches or pants in Bible times, whereas women did not. In Exodus 28 God gave instructions for the priests, and in verse 42 they were to "make them linen breeches to cover their nakedness; from the loins even unto the thighs they shall reach." The breeches were pants that were worn under the priest's robe. Obviously these were different from the pants men wear today, but the point is that they were an item of dress worn only by men. All of the priests were male. Women, on the other hand, were never instructed to wear breeches of any kind in ancient times.

The point is that the dress of women and the dress of men were distinctively different in Israel. The fact that their clothing styles were different then than those of our day is irrelevant. We have the Bible's principles in these matters, and they are applicable to every time and place.

We don't live in that bygone era. We must therefore carefully apply the principles of Scripture to our own age and situation.

I ONLY WEAR FEMININE PANTS.

In his excellent book "The Fall and Rise of Christian Standards," David Kidd answers this as follows:

> "Do you remember when 'lady's pants' first came out? They zipped up the side. Today you would be hard pressed to find a pair of jeans, or any other pants in the ladies department that did not zip up the front. The reason for a zipper up the front of men's pants is anatomically obvious, but for women? Would the same argument many women use to justify their 'lady's' jeans be accepted if their husbands used its reverse as a defense for wearing a skirt or dress? Don't laugh. Way back in the 1980s, a popular afternoon talk show host had a guest on his TV program who was modeling and marketing a man's skirt, complete with a zipper in the front and pockets in the back. My dear

Christian lady, if you will defend your ladies pants, upon what basis will you object to a man's dress?"

I ONLY WEAR MODEST PANTS.

Some women agree with us on every issue of modesty we have discussed except for the unisex aspect of pants, believing that female pants are no longer directly identified with the unisex movement and that it is proper for a Christian woman to wear pants as long as they are modest.

So let's leave the unisex aspect aside for a moment and discuss this.

The first point I would make is that it is highly doubtful whether any pants on a woman are truly modest. While loose pants on a woman are most assuredly more modest than tight jeans, and my survey of men proved that, they still show off the woman's rear end in a way that a modest dress does not, and they accentuate the crotch area and draw people's attention there as no dress does.

Note the following comments by men and women who have written to me on this subject:

One woman said: "I never have felt comfortable wearing pants, whether they were women's clothing or men's clothing. That was never the real issue of the reason I gave up wearing anything that looked like trousers. Anything that brought attention to certain parts of my body bothered me."

Another lady said: "My husband told me that in his opinion, MOST women's pants are immodest, because they are form-fitting and show the woman's shape, especially the derriere."

Another said: "A good argument against a woman wearing pants is that they aren't modest. They show one's private lines in the crotch area, hardly modest. They also show ones hip lines, also not modest. We still cannot get this across to our members, many of which wear jeans and just don't understand that their shape is well evident, especially from the back. These are not young, slight teens, these are overweight adult women with three or more children under their belt, so to speak, and I look no better than they, but I sure wouldn't willingly embarrass myself by forcing people to look at it. A nice, long, flouncy dress hides this nicely."

The female authors of *Dress: The Heart of the Matter* said: "Should women wear pants? No! In fact, wearing pants accents or draws attention to the pelvic and hip area of the lady, areas only her husband should see. A dress does not draw attention to this area unless it is too tight and formfitting" (Shirley Starr and Lori Waltemyer, *Dress: The Heart of the Matter*, p. 37).

One man said, "While it is true that some things on your list will draw your attention quicker and cause you to look longer, even 'looser-fitting pants' direct a man's gaze to the area of the hips."

Another man described the following experience.

> "A few years ago, I preached a message about standards (including music, dress, and others). I asked for a show of hands as to how many men would admit their eyes were drawn to a woman's crotch when she wore pants instead of a skirt or dress. More than two dozen hands went up (and who knows how many more were hesitant to make the public confession with their wives right next to them?). The group included many of the finest Christians I know, some of whom are ordained ministers and missionaries."

There is, then, a distinct possibility that female pants are not perfectly modest in any of their incarnations.

Second, wearing pants for a woman is a questionable standard. If it were not questionable why do many Christian men have a conviction that it is wrong? The child of God should not allow himself or herself to pursue questionable things.

Third, wearing pants identifies one with modern female fashions and leads to the perpetual temptation to wear tight pants. The Christian woman who is convinced that pants can be a modest and proper attire is constantly tempted to push the boundaries pertaining to the style of her dress, because of the pressure from the fashion industry.

Fourth, it is exceedingly rare that a woman will maintain a strong conviction about modest dress and maintain the highest standard in this realm if she wears pants. In my experience, the woman who wears loose pants will wear tighter ones. Further, even if she has a true conviction about always wearing her pants in a loose, non form-fitting style, her daughters do not follow her example. I have never seen or heard of a case of a Christian woman living in a Western culture that had a true spiritual conviction about only wearing "modest" pants and stood by that conviction consistently and trained her daughters to have the same conviction. Wearing pants, any style of pants, simply does not go hand-in-hand with strong convictions about modesty.

Finally, I would ask you to give the issue of offense serious consideration. There are literally hundreds of thousands of men in fundamentalist churches (tens of thousands of whom I have preached to and hundreds of whom I know personally) who have a conviction that women should not wear pants, that it is a unisex statement at best and less than proper even when the style is loose. Would it not be scriptural and godly to forego offending these men of God even if you think they are wrong? Is wearing pants something to live and die for? Is it so important that you don't care who you offend? The apostle Paul said, "Wherefore, if meat make my brother to offend, I will eat no flesh while the world standeth, lest I make my brother to offend" (1 Cor. 8:13).

PREACHERS THAT PREACH AGAINST PANTS ARE MEAN-SPIRITED AND THEY JUST WANT TO DICTATE HOW I DRESS.

Preachers are just men. They are sinners (hopefully) saved by grace. There probably are mean-spirited preachers who do not preach standards of modesty for the benefit of the people but just because they are dictatorial, and that is wrong. Such a man should not be in the ministry.

I can't speak for other preachers, but I can speak for myself, and I can testify before God that my motive in preaching godly dress standards for Christians is to please the Lord and to be a blessing to His churches and to see righteousness increased in a wicked world. God has called me to preach His Word, and that means all of the Word. If I were to leave off preaching the passages that we have covered in this book I would be an unfaithful preacher.

God being my witness, by preaching these things I am not trying to hurt anyone or to take away anything that is good. I am trying to help God's people be a godly light in a dark world and to escape the bondage of the world, the flesh, and the Devil. To get people to separate from this wicked world is a blessing to them, to their children, to their grandchildren, to their friends and neighbors, and to their churches.

WEARING DRESSES IS AN OLD FASHIONED THING; WE SHOULD TRY TO BE FASHIONABLE SO WE DON'T LOOK ODD AND BE THOUGHT OF AS WEIRD. FURTHERMORE, NO ONE WEARS DRESSES ANYMORE AND OTHERS MOCK ME WHEN I TRY TO WEAR THEM.

The Bible does not instruct God's people to be fashionable but to be holy and separate apart for the Lord and pleasing to Him. We are not to be conformed to the world (Romans 12:2).

God's people are to be peculiar unto Him because of their redemption and by their zeal for holy living (Titus 2:14).

God's people are to bear the reproach of Christ in this wicked world and not be ashamed of Him (Mark 8:38; 2 Timothy 2:12; Hebrews 13:13).

Philippians 2:15-16 says that we reach the world by being blameless and by living different from its crooked and perverse ways. This is how we shine as lights in this dark world. When God's people adopt the world's fashions they are no longer light and salt.

IT SEEMS TO ME THAT WOMEN WHO WEAR DRESSES LOOK DOWN ON WOMEN WHO WEAR PANTS.

This is doubtless a great exaggeration. There are many godly and humble women who wear dresses and do not look down on women who do not have that conviction. Many of them can remember when they themselves did not have this conviction, and they are merciful and patient toward those who are struggling with dress issues.

Even if some women who wear dresses do look down on women who wear pants, that does not mean that wearing dresses is wrong. There are hypocrites in the churches, but that does not mean that the church is wrong. It is still God's program in this age and "the pillar and ground of the truth" (1 Tim. 3:15).

It is also true that some women who wear pants look down on those who wear dresses! In fact, practically every woman who wrote to share her testimony about how the Lord convicted her not to wear pants told me that she has been ridiculed for this by female relatives and acquaintances. Typical was one lady who said, "My daughter and I started wearing dresses just last November. I've been laughed at by other Christians and have had a lot of things said to me."

SOME PANTS ARE MORE MODEST THAN SOME DRESSES

While it might be true that some pants are more modest than some dresses or skirts, that is not a good excuse for wearing pants. The Christian's goal should not be just to get by but to choose the most excellent things before the Lord (Phil. 1:9-10).

We have shown that pants are not as modest as modest dresses and that pants also have the problem of being associated with unisex fashion and the feminist movement, whereas dresses do not have this stigma.

The proper solution to the matter of an immodest dress or skirt is not any kind of pants but a truly modest dress!

PANTS ARE MORE COMFORTABLE AND ARE EASIER FOR ME TO GET INTO.

The answer to this argument is that comfort and ease are not the standards for Christian living. The objective of the born-again Christian who loves the Lord is to please His Master in all things and to bring glory to Him. Such a Christian knows that he was bought with a great price and that he was redeemed to live a holy life in this present world (Titus 2:11-13). He knows that he is called to die to self and to endure hardness as a good soldier of Jesus Christ (2 Timothy 2:3). If a soldier told his superior officer that he didn't want to wear the uniform because it isn't comfortable to him, he would be scorned, and if he persisted he would be disciplined.

I MIGHT LOSE MY JOB OR NOT GET A JOB IF I REFUSE TO WEAR THE WORLD'S DRESS STYLES

In Matthew 6:33 Jesus taught, "But seek ye first the kingdom of God, and his righteousness; and all these things shall be added unto you."

This is a far-reaching truth and it contains a wonderful promise. If I put God first, He will take care of me.

I have been saved for 33 years and during 14 of those I worked in a "secular occupation." But from the beginning of my Christian life I determined that I would put God first in my work and not take any job that would hinder my

Christian life or make it impossible for me to obey the Bible's precepts. One of those precepts, for example, is not forsaking the assembling of ourselves together (Heb. 10:25). I have determined not to take a job that would keep me out of church, and the Lord has honored that and has always taken care of me and provided jobs that did not force me to have to choose between God and mammon.

The same promise is available to the woman who wants to dress modestly. If you will determine in your heart that under no circumstance are you going to disobey the Lord's precepts, not even for the sake of a job, He will surely take care of you.

Further, if you get a job at a place where the females usually dress in pants or some other attire that does not fit the Bible's definition of modesty, and you determine to dress in a feminine and modest manner in that situation, you can be a powerful witness. One woman said, "I know a girl who went to work at a fast food place in a skirt and was able to witness to everyone there, because they kept asking her about her religion--because of the skirt."

I DON'T HAVE ANY MONEY TO BUY NEW CLOTHES

Matthew 6:33 is a good promise for this problem, as well. "But seek ye first the kingdom of God, and his righteousness; and all these things shall be added unto you." The Lord Jesus challenges us to put God and His will first in our lives, and He encourages us that if we do this God will take care of us.

The following testimony demonstrates how faithful God is to keep His promises:

> 'I have said before that after getting saved I began to search the Scriptures and read everything I could get my hands on to learn God's will for my life, i.e., mother, wife, child of God. It wasn't long before God blessed me with some very dear Christian friends to replace the ungodly ones I had walked away from. I remember one day while with a wonderful lady, I asked her, 'Candy, don't you ever wear

pants?' She (with a funny smile on her face), said, 'Chris, are you sure you really want to know that?' I look back at that day now and just have to laugh. I wanted so to serve God, to be the PECULIAR people He talks of in His Word. So she proceeded to show me in the Word why I never saw her in pants -- because God said it is wrong -- well being a young Christian and wanting to 'do right in all things' I went home packed away the daisy duke shorts, halters, short skirts (remember this was the 80's folks!). Well, once I did that there was nothing to wear. So I called this dear friend and told her I didn't know what to do. She promptly went to the thrift shop and, bless her heart, brought over the ugliest dress I had ever seen! (I'm sure she thought it was perfect for me.)

"You're probably asking yourself right about now why didn't I go out and buy new clothes. Well, there was no money!

"Anyway, I wore that dress and a skirt I got from my mom for nearly two weeks. Inside I wanted to do it for the right reason, but I came to the place that I missed my 'old' clothes. I talked to my husband about it and he said (with great wisdom), 'Chris, I think you made the right decision, but don't do it for me or because of Candy; it's up to you.' Well I kept wearing dresses and skirts for a week or two more, mostly because I was afraid that Candy or her husband would think badly of me if I didn't.

"But then one morning I closed the door and promptly jumped into my shorts and tee. I had no problem doing that, HOWEVER, when I looked into the mirror I was ashamed! God had done a work in my heart. I knew then and there I would not be able to leave that room in those clothes. Praise the Lord. For the rest of my days I would do it for Him! ...

"Want to hear the best part? The very day I surrendered that area of my life to God He showered me with a blessing I never would have dreamed of. This same lady, who had no idea of what I was going through (but God knew, amen!), brought over two huge bags of clothes. There were jean skirts galore, nice too, and jumpers, oh what a blessing that was! I about had a shoutin' fit!" (http://www.momof9splace.com/modesty.html).

I BELIEVE THAT THOSE WHO PREACH ON "MODESTY" ARE LEGALISTIC.

Though we are saved by grace *without* works, we are saved *unto* good works (Eph. 2:8-10).

The grace of God that saved us also teaches us "that, denying ungodliness and worldly lusts, we should live soberly, righteously, and godly, in this present world" (Titus 2:11-12).

It is not legalism for a blood-washed believer to preach the whole counsel of God (Acts 20:27) and to strive to obey God in every area of his or her life. The Lord Jesus Christ commanded that His people train the baptized converts to "observe ALL things whatsoever I have commanded you" (Matt. 28:20).

True legalism is to teach that salvation is by works or by grace *plus* works. This was the error of the false teachers in Galatia (Gal. 1:6-9; 2:16-21; 3:1-3). Legalism is also to add man's tradition to the level of the Word of God. This was one of the errors of the Pharisees (Mat. 15:1-9).

Strict obedience to God's Word for the born-again Christian is the way of liberty, not bondage.

> "Then said Jesus to those Jews which believed on him, If ye continue in my word, then are ye my disciples indeed; and ye shall know the truth, and the truth shall make you free" (John 8:31-32).

THE BIBLE SAYS WE SHOULD NOT JUDGE, DOESN'T IT?

It is wrong to make a blanket statement that Christians are not supposed to judge. The Bible forbids certain types of judging and commends other types. The Lord Jesus forbade hypocritical judging in Matthew 7:1-5, but He commended judging false teachers in Matthew 7:15. Romans 14:4-5 warns us not to judge one another in matters of Christian liberty such as in diet and keeping of holy days. In other words, we are not to judge if the Bible is silent. But in 1 Corinthians 14:29 God's people are commanded to judge preaching and in Ephesians 5:11 Christians are commanded to reprove the works of darkness. That involves judging which things are the works of darkness and which are not. Paul judged Peter and reproved him publicly for his hypocrisy (Gal. 2:11-14). Paul judged the sin at the church of Corinth (1 Cor. 5:3). Paul said Christians will judge the world and angels and should therefore judge things in the church (1 Cor. 6:1-5). Paul even taught that Christian love involves judgment. "And this I pray, that your love may abound yet more and more in knowledge and in all judgment" (Phil. 1:9). Further, "he that is spiritual judgeth all things" (1 Cor. 2:16). The spiritual man does not judge by his own thinking but by the Word of God. He knows that he lives in a dark world and He knows that he has the truth in the Scriptures, and he wisely judges everything by this Standard.

WHAT ABOUT THE ISSUE OF MODESTY IN OTHER CULTURES? NOT EVERY CULTURE WEARS PANTS AND DRESSES.

The answer to this is that the Bible's principles of dress apply to any time and place. The three great principles are chastity, distinction, and identification. These can be applied to dress in Africa, South America, Asia, or any other part of the world.

My wife and I have spent many years as missionaries in South Asia. The culture is radically different from that in North America, yet the principles of the Bible are perfectly workable in either place. The men commonly wear pants and dress-style shirts and they like to be neat and clean, so there is usually no issue on that side unless we have a convert from the drug culture who wears his hair long or some such thing. In that case we have to teach them not to follow western rock fashions. The women commonly wear either a sari or a khurta sudiwal. The sari consists of a blouse and a long cloth wrapped around the woman's body. It is feminine attire that is never worn by a man, and, like a dress, it can be modest or immodest. The sari can be wrapped too tightly, and the blouse can be too tight, too high, too low, or too open in the back. My wife teaches the women how to wear saris in a modest manner. The khurta sudiwal usually consists of silk pants (the sudiwal) worn under a dress-like garment (the khurta) that hangs down to the thighs or the knees or lower. It is usually accompanied by a long scarf that is draped around the neck and down the back. The dress part is slit on the sides but the slit does not slow any part of the woman's legs. It can be modest if the dress part is long enough and not too tight and the slit is not very high and the pants underneath are not too tight. In the past 15 years western dress styles have had a growing influence in this part of the world and we now have to teach the younger women not to wear western style pants and such, which we did not have to worry about previously.

When it comes to identification, the Christians in a Hindu or Buddhist culture have to be careful that their clothing does not associate them with idolatry. Hindu women, for example, wear red saris in their worship, so our female converts avoid wearing them so as not to be identified with idolatry. One new believer recently told my wife that she had given away her red saris, because that was her "old life." Hindu men wear a "holy string" underneath their shirts, and Christian men are careful to put that away.

WHAT ABOUT TATTOOS AND PIERCINGS?

A survey in Canada found that "75% of young conservative Christians believe tattooing is a valid spiritual expression" ("For the Love of God," *The Vancouver Sun*, Vancouver, British Columbia, February 1999).

Reporter Douglas Todd of *The Vancouver Sun* visited the Vineyard Christian Fellowship in Langley, British Columbia, and found that tattoos are the newest "in thing" for Vineyard Christians. Amy Bonde, who is a staff member at the Vineyard in Langley, has a large Celtic cross tattooed on the small of her back. Encircling the cross are Hebrew letters that allegedly mean, "I am my beloved's, and he is mine." Bonde says the tattoo signifies that she looks upon Jesus Christ as her "lover."

The Vancouver Sun report notes that the TATTOOING REPRESENTS "A SIGN OF A SEISMIC SHIFT IN EVANGELICAL CHRISTIANITY, which has been associated for most of this century with harsh rules about controlling one's body: no long hair on men, no pants on women, no drinking, no dancing, no jewelry and certainly no tattooing."

The *Bismarck Tribune* (North Dakota) ran an article in November 1998 about the Christian Tattoo Association operated by Randy Mastre and two other members of New Song Community Church in Bismarck. Their goal is "to bring Christianity to tattooers."

What is wrong with "Christian" tattooing?

First of all, the Old Testament plainly forbade tattooing.

> "Ye shall not make any cuttings in your flesh for the dead, nor print any marks upon you: I am the LORD" (Lev. 19:28).

> "They shall not make baldness upon their head, neither shall they shave off the corner of their beard, nor make any cuttings in their flesh" (Lev. 21:5).

This is such a clear command, that one would need a compelling reason to disregard it, even though it is an Old Testament law.

In some cases we are told in the New Testament that something in the Old is not for us. That is true for the Old Testament dietary laws (Rom. 14:2-3; 1 Tim. 4:1-5) and for the sabbath (Col. 2:16), but there is no such statement in regard to tattooing.

For a Christian to get a tattoo would be to say that he or she can be certain that what God was concerned about in Leviticus 19:28 and 21:5 He no longer cares about, and I don't see what basis of interpretation allows that.

Second, God's people are not to be identified with evil.

God forbade the Israelites to cut their flesh because it was an identification with paganism and idolatry, and the New Testament contains the same principles and restrictions.

> "Abstain from all appearance of evil" (1 Thessalonians 5:22).

> "And have no fellowship with the unfruitful works of darkness, but rather reprove them" (Ephesians 5:11).

> "I beseech you therefore, brethren, by the mercies of God, that ye present your bodies a living sacrifice, holy, acceptable unto God, which is your reasonable service. And be not conformed to this world..." (Romans 12:1-2).

> "But I say, that the things which the Gentiles sacrifice, they sacrifice to devils, and not to God: and I would not that ye should have fellowship with devils. Ye cannot drink the cup of the Lord, and the cup of devils: ye cannot be partakers of the Lord's table, and of the table of devils. Do we provoke the Lord to jealousy? are we stronger than he?" (1 Corinthians 10:20-22).

Tattooing is still intimately associated with idolatry, paganism, moral debauchery, and rebellion.

An article by Clay Thompson in the Pacific News Service for July 27, 1996, was titled "Pagan Fashion's New Frontier - Facial Tattoos." Note that the author, who in this article makes no claim to be a Christian, associates tattoos with paganism. He connects it with a "new reverence for pagan beliefs."

A prominent book on tattooing is *Pagan Fleshworks*. It is by Maureen Mercury and contains photos by Steve Haworth, identified as "the foremost body modification artist in the United States." "Body modification" is the practice of burning, inking, cutting, piercing, and otherwise desecrating one's God-given body.

A July 2003 survey of more than 2,000 people in the United States, reported in the AFP for Oct. 11, found that among women who get tattoos, 34% "feel sexier," and 29% overall "FEEL MORE REBELLIOUS." One woman interviewed by the *Vancouver Sun* admitted that she got a tattoo "PARTLY OUT OF REBELLION against the normal Christian stereotype of 'You can't do this, you can't do that.'" She admits that her mother did not want her to get a tattoo and did not like it ("For the Love of God," *The Vancouver Sun*, Vancouver, British Columbia, Feb. 1999). Another Vineyard member, Peter Davyduck, who has a tattoo of the word "SIN" on his ankle, says this is a message to "judgmental Christians that everyone is a sinner and should be accepted in spite of it." Note the rebellious attitude in this statement. Every born-again Bible-believing Christian knows that everyone is a sinner, but this does not mean that it does not matter how professing Christians should live.

Such rebellion is forbidden in God's Word. 1 Peter 4:5 says, "Likewise, ye younger, submit yourselves unto the elder. Yea, all of you be subject one to another, and be clothed with humility: for God resisteth the proud, and giveth grace to the humble." And Ephesians 5:21 says, "Submitting yourselves one to another in the fear of God."

A young woman who got tattoos before she was saved told me that tattooing is addictive. Wherein is the addiction?

A third reason against tattoos is that the Bible warns the Christian not to cause moral offence and cause of spiritual stumbling.

> "Give none offence, neither to the Jews, nor to the Gentiles, nor to the church of God" (1 Cor. 10:32).

> "Giving no offence in any thing, that the ministry be not blamed" (2 Cor. 6:3).

> "Wherefore, if meat make my brother to offend, I will eat no flesh while the world standeth, lest I make my brother to offend" (1 Cor. 8:10).

This was one of the apostle Paul's guiding principles. He did not want his actions to cause someone to be offended and to stumble spiritually. For this purpose, he was willing even to forego lawful things such as eating meat. How much more should Christians in this age forego highly questionable things such as tattooing and pants on women and "Christian" rock for the sake of being a blessing and encouragement to their conservative brethren! But, sadly, the Christian rock-tattooing culture comes decked out with the rock & roll attitude of "no one is going to take away my fun; I'm not going to let some old fogy tell me what to do."

This is an unscriptural attitude, to say the least. What if a professing Christian follows the example of the "Christian tattoo crowd" and gets involved in the tattoo culture and is drawn into sin?

Not only is the Christian to avoid things that are obviously evil, but he is to avoid things that would cause offense to others even if those things are in not necessarily wrong in themselves:

> "It is good neither to eat flesh, nor to drink wine, nor any thing whereby thy brother stumbleth, or is offended, or is made weak" (Romans 14:21).

The Christian is to live his life to please others instead of himself. Contemporary-style Christians, though, do not care if they offend others with their rock music and worldly appearance. They protest that they have liberty to do as they please. This is carnal rebellion, and it is the attitude that lies at the heart of apostasy. Those who desire to throw off restrictions on their lifestyles are not following the Bible but their own self-willed lusts. They are fulfilling 2 Timothy 4:3-4:

"For the time will come when they will not endure sound doctrine; but AFTER THEIR OWN LUSTS shall they heap to themselves teachers, having itching ears; And they shall turn away their ears from the truth, and shall be turned unto fables."

A final reason against tattooing is that the believer's body is not his own; it is the temple of the Holy Spirit.

"What? know ye not that your body is the temple of the Holy Ghost which is in you, which ye have of God, and ye are not your own?" (1 Corinthians 6:19).

For the born-again Christian, tattooing is graffiti on someone's else's temple.

The following is a testimony of Pastor Charlie Haddad who got tattoos before he was saved:
"I was a professing Christian for 24 Years (Catholic) and growing up I was hanging out with some Muslim friends. Some of them got tattoos of a sword and the moon. I then thought I wanted to get a cross and the face of Jesus, and I did, one on each shoulder. Looking back I got them out of pride, it was more of religious pride. I was a Christian only by name, thinking these tattoos would identify me as a Christian, far from it, I didn't know the Lord. Had I really known the Lord and wanted to walk in His ways and the way of His Word I would have obeyed Him and written His Word upon my heart and not on my body. I would have memorised and mediated on His Word instead of having a form of godliness (Proverbs 3:3; 7:2-2). I regret getting these tattoos, and I am ashamed. I know it is not pleasing to the Lord."

LOVE IS MORE IMPORTANT THAN STANDARDS OF LIVING, ISN'T IT?

When Bible-believing Christians take the Word of God seriously and preach the whole counsel of God, including those parts on separation and modesty, they are invariably charged with a lack of love. A woman wrote to me and said:

> "You preach about heresy. WHAT ABOUT LOVE? ...
> What you call 'zeal for the Bible' I call arrogance and pride.
> If you knew the Bible as well as you claim, then I believe
> you'd live it. The lost will never be reached through SUCH
> HATRED" (Letter from a reader, May 1997).

This lady was upset about my preaching and charged me with a lack of love, and this in spite of her own haughty and incredibly judgmental attitude! To this generation, the negative aspects of biblical Christianity are unloving. To carefully test things by the Bible is a lack of compassion. To mark and avoid false teachers is hatemongering. To preach high and holy standards of Christian living is legalism. To warn of false gospels and to discipline heretics is mean-spirited.

A few years ago, evangelist Jack Van Impe, a former fundamentalist, rejected biblical separatism and went over to the contemporary philosophy. He said: "Till I die I will proclaim nothing but love for all my brothers and sisters in Christ, my Catholic brothers and sisters, Protestant brothers and sisters, Christian Reformed, Lutherans, I don't care what label you are. By this shall all men know that ye are my disciples if ye have love one to another."

This is the popular view of love, but it is false and dangerous.

First of all this view does not understand the definition of true Christian love.

Love is crucial, of course. The Bible says that without love "I am become as sounding brass, or a tinkling cymbal." The

Bible tells us that God is love and those who know God will reflect His love.

What is love, though? "Love" to human thinking is a warm feeling or a sensual romantic thought. "Love" to the contemporary Christian generation is broadmindedness and non-judgmental tolerance of anyone that claims to love the Lord. This is not what the Bible says about love. Consider the following verses of Scripture:

> "Jesus answered and said unto him, IF A MAN LOVE ME, HE WILL KEEP MY WORDS: and my Father will love him, and we will come unto him, and make our abode with him" (John 14:23).

> "And this I pray, that your LOVE MAY ABOUND YET MORE AND MORE IN KNOWLEDGE AND IN ALL JUDGMENT; That ye may approve things that are excellent; that ye may be sincere and without offence till the day of Christ" (Philippians 1:9-10).

> "For THIS IS THE LOVE OF GOD, THAT WE KEEP HIS COMMANDMENTS: and his commandments are not grievous" (1 John 5:3).

Biblical love is obedience to God and His Word. Love is not a warm fuzzy feeling. It is not blissful romanticism. For a woman to love her husband means she submits to and serves him according to the Bible. For a man to love his wife means he treats her in the way the Bible commands. For children to love their parents means they honor and obey them as the Bible commands. Love is obedience to God's Word.

Christian love is not an emotion, though emotion is closely associated with it. It is not non-judgmentalism. It is not non-critical acceptance of and tolerance of things that are wrong. Biblical love is vigilant. It is based on knowledge and judgment from God's Word. It proves all things, and it approves only those things that reflect the will of God.

Secondly, those who hold the contemporary view are also confused about the direction of love.

The first direction of love must be toward God. When discussing these matters, those who hold the contemporary philosophy talk much about love of man, but what about the love of God? According to the Lord Jesus Christ, what is the greatest commandment?

> "Then one of them, which was a lawyer, asked him a question, tempting him, and saying, Master, which is the great commandment in the law? Jesus said unto him, Thou shalt love the Lord thy God with all thy heart, and with all thy soul, and with all thy mind. This is the first and great commandment. And the second is like unto it, Thou shalt love thy neighbour as thyself" (Mat. 22:35-39).

The first and great commandment is NOT to love one's neighbor. That is the second commandment. The first and great commandment is to love God with all the heart, soul, and mind.

Some point their fingers at the Bible-believing fundamentalist and charge him with a lack of love toward men because he exercises judgment and discipline and separation. What, though, about love for God and His Word? Some tell me that I need to love women so much that I won't hurt their feelings about what they wear. I reply that I need to love God and His Truth first, and that means that I will obey the Bible, and that means I will preach all of it and not just part of it. A genuine love for God requires that I care more about God's Word and God's will than about men and their feelings and opinions and programs.

The direction of love not only must be toward God but it must also be toward those who are in danger. The contemporary crowd tells me that I need to love the worldly people and not preach so as to offend them, but they are largely silent on the subject of love for those who are ensnared by the Devil and the world and the flesh. The fact is that we love people enough to warn of immodesty and every

160

other form of immorality and lasciviousness so that they can escape that trap if they are willing to heed the warning. I thank the Lord for the hundreds and hundreds of people who have contacted me and thanked me for my strong preaching because it has changed their lives; it has convinced them of sins and errors that they need to repent of; it has encouraged them to walk in God's straight and narrow path rather than the broad way of destruction. They have thanked me because the preaching helped them live holy lives and helped them raise their children in a godly way and helped them find churches where they could find nurture and protection from the world.

A shepherd who loves wolves more than the sheep is a confused and wicked shepherd.

ISN'T IT PHARISAICAL TO MAKE RULES ABOUT DRESS?

"Phariseeism" is a term frequently used to describe Bible-believing Christians who are zealous for pure doctrine and who desire to maintain holy standards of living in this wicked hour. This "free thinking" attitude was expressed at a "Christian" rock concert called Greenbelt '83: "We don't believe in a fundamentalist approach. We don't set ground rules. Our teaching is non-directive. We want to encourage people to make their own choices."

But what is a Pharisee? The Pharisee's error was not his love for the truth and his zeal for biblical righteousness. The Pharisee did not love the truth; he loved his own man-made tradition (Mt. 15:1-9). If the Pharisee had loved the truth, he would have loved Jesus Christ (Jn. 8:47)! The Pharisee did not love God's righteousness; he loved his own self-righteousness (Lk. 18:9-14). The Pharisee did not have a zeal for God; he had a zeal for his own false religion (Mt. 23:15). The Pharisee did not preach salvation by grace; he preached salvation by the law (Mat. 12:7). The Pharisee did not believe in regeneration but in mere external reformation (Lk. 11:59).

161

To call the fundamentalist Bible-believing Christian who is saved by the grace of Jesus Christ and who knows that he is only an unworthy sinner worthy of God's wrath and therefore is not self-righteous and who loves the precious Word of God and wants to please God in all things a Pharisee, is a vicious slander.

By the way, until recently most evangelical and fundamentalist churches and Bible Colleges had a dress code, forbade rock music, dancing, etc. Were all of our forefathers Pharisees?

For example, the *New York Times* for January 28, 2007, ran an article entitled "The First Dance," about the first dance allowed in the history of John Brown University in December 2006. For nearly 90 years this Christian school, located in Siloam Springs, Arkansas, considered dancing a worldly activity and forbade it. In this present "contemporary" age, though, such taboos are old-fashioned, legalistic, even Pharisaical. John Brown University was founded in 1919 by a Salvation Army preacher. The same thing has happened in recent years at many other Christian schools, including Wheaton College, BIOLA, Cornerstone University, and Baylor University. When we preach against these things today and say that modern dancing is worldly and Christian women should dress modestly, we are condemned as legalists and Pharisees. It makes me wonder. Were all of our evangelical and fundamentalist Christian forefathers Pharisees? Fifty years ago the vast majority of them believed the same thing on these issues as we believe today. As the *New York Times* observed, "Until last October, dancing had been seen at J.B.U. as a gateway to sin." Since it is obvious that modern dancing has not gotten godlier in the past 90 years, something else must have changed and that something else is the gross worldliness of evangelicalism and even fundamentalism today.

ISN'T THE SINCERITY OF THE HEART THE IMPORTANT THING?

Those who defend the contemporary Christian philosophy with its worldly standard of dress often argue that the only thing that matters is whether or not a person is sincere.

We would answer this, first of all, by reminding our readers of the deceptive nature of man's heart.

> "The heart is deceitful above all things, and desperately wicked: who can know it?" (Jeremiah 17:9).

> "He that trusteth in his own heart is a fool: but whoso walketh wisely, he shall be delivered" (Proverbs 28:26).

> "There is a way which seemeth right unto a man, but the end thereof are the ways of death" (Proverbs 14:12).

These verses remind us that man's heart cannot be trusted. It is possible for a person to deceive himself and others. It is therefore impossible to know whether or not someone is sincerely seeking to please God. It is impossible to know for sure whether or not a person has sincere motives for doing what they do. Man's heart is complex, and he often has many motives for what he does.

Second, God requires obedience to His Word and does not accept man's sincere disobedience. There are many examples of this in the Bible. Moses was very sincere before God, but when he struck the rock instead of speaking to it, God judged him and refused to allow him to enter Canaan (Num. 20:7-14). There is no question that Moses was sincere when he struck the rock, but God did not accept his sincere and earnest disobedience. When Aaron's sons offered strange fire, God struck them dead, paying no attention to whether or not they were acting sincerely (Lev. 10:1-7). When Saul disobeyed in the seemingly minor matter of refusing to destroy all of the cattle belonging to the Amalekites, God judged him and removed the kingdom from him (1 Samuel 15). Saul protested that he had done the deed in the sincerity

163

of his heart, but this did not change God's mind. When Uzzah steadied the cart holding the ark, God struck him dead (1 Sam. 6:6-7). It appears from the record that Uzzah was sincerely trying to assist in the service of God, but God did not accept it because it was not done according to His Word.

Third, the Bible says that the Christian race must be run according to the divine rule or there is no reward from God.

> "And if a man also strive for masteries, yet is he not crowned, except he strive lawfully" (2 Tim. 2:5).

This was one reason why Paul exercised his life and ministry so carefully and strictly.

> "Know ye not that they which run in a race run all, but one receiveth the prize? So run, that ye may obtain. And every man that striveth for the mastery is temperate in all things. Now they do it to obtain a corruptible crown; but we an incorruptible. I therefore so run, not as uncertainly; so fight I, not as one that beateth the air: but I keep under my body, and bring it into subjection: lest that by any means, when I have preached to others, I myself should be a castaway" (1 Cor. 9:24-27).

It is obvious that sincerity and earnestness in the service of Christ, while a good thing, is not enough. I must run the Christian race according to the Word of God or God does not accept my service.

ISN'T CHRISTIANITY ALL ABOUT GRACE?

Grace is certainly at the heart of biblical Christianity. The true Gospel is called "the grace of Christ" (Galatians 1:6). The grace of God, though, does not produce license; it produces holiness and a zeal for good works. Consider the following important passage of Scripture:

> "For THE GRACE OF GOD that bringeth salvation hath appeared to all men, TEACHING US THAT, DENYING UNGODLINESS AND WORLDLY LUSTS, WE SHOULD

LIVE SOBERLY, RIGHTEOUSLY, AND GODLY, IN THIS PRESENT WORLD; Looking for that blessed hope, and the glorious appearing of the great God and our Saviour Jesus Christ; Who gave himself for us, that he might redeem us from all iniquity, and purify unto himself a peculiar people, zealous of good works" (Titus 2:11-14).

The grace of God teaches men to deny worldly lusts. The "grace" so frequently mentioned by those who hold the contemporary philosophy is not biblical grace because it does not produce separation from worldliness. It does not produce peculiar people; it produces worldly people who are religious. It is more akin to license than to true biblical grace.

> "For, brethren, ye have been called unto liberty; only use not liberty for an occasion to the flesh, but by love serve one another" (Gal. 5:13).

DIDN'T PAUL TEACH THAT ALL THINGS ARE LAWFUL FOR THE CHRISTIAN?

Many misuse Paul's statement in 1 Corinthians 6:12 and 10:23, "All things are lawful unto me...," as an excuse for wearing what they please.

We have examined 1 Corinthians 6:12-13 and 1 Corinthians 10:23-24 under the section on "Biblical Modesty in the New Testament."

DIDN'T PAUL SAY HE WAS MADE ALL THINGS TO ALL MEN; DOESN'T THAT MEAN THAT WE SHOULD LIVE SO THAT UNBELIEVERS DO NOT FEEL UNCOMFORTABLE AROUND US?

In 1 Corinthians 9:22 Paul said, "To the weak became I as weak, that I might gain the weak: I am made all things to all men, that I might by all means save some."

If this were isolated from the rest of Scripture one could assume that Paul was willing to do anything whatsoever to reach the lost, including adopting their appearance and lifestyle. This is a doctrine that is popular among the "rock & roll Christian" crowd today.

However, when one compares Scripture with Scripture, we find that Paul did not mean this. In 1 Corinthians 9:21, for example, he says, "To them that are without law, as without law, (BEING NOT WITHOUT LAW TO GOD, BUT UNDER THE LAW TO CHRIST,) that I might gain them that are without law." Thus, he explains that he was always under the law to Christ and was never free to do anything contrary to the Scriptures. For example, Paul would never have adopted long hair in order to reach the heathen, because Christ's law says long hair on a man is shameful (1 Cor. 11:14). Paul would never have conformed in any way to the world, because Christ's law forbids this (Rom. 12:2). He would never have allowed any of the Christian women working with him to adopt Corinth's immodest dress fashions, because Christ's law forbids this (Rom. 12:2; 1 Tim. 2:9, 1 John 2:15-16, etc.).

Further, a few verses along in the same passage Paul says, "But I keep under my body, and bring it into subjection: lest that by any means, when I have preached to others, I myself should be a castaway" (1 Cor. 9:27). Thus, Paul was always strict in regard to what he allowed himself to do and he would not have done anything spiritually carelessness or "borderline." He would never, therefore, have condoned immodest dress on females because of the potential that he or some other man would be brought under bondage to sexual lust and its potential consequences.

And in Galatians 5:13 Paul says, "For, brethren, ye have been called unto liberty; only use not liberty for an occasion to the flesh, but by love serve one another." Thus, Paul's liberty was not the liberty to serve the flesh in any way.

Paul taught that believers are to "abstain from all appearance of evil" (1 Thess. 5:22). That is the strictest form of separation. Not only did Paul avoid every type of evil but even the very appearance of evil.

We agree with the following statement by Iain Murray:

"The Christian faith is rather at its strongest when its antagonism to unbelief is most definite, when its spirit is other-worldly, and when its whole trust is not 'in the wisdom of men but in the power of God' (1 Cor. 2:5)" (Murray, *Evangelicalism Divided*, 2000, p. 212).

Testimonies From Christian Women on the Issue of Modest Dress

The following are some of the testimonies I have received from Christian women about how they were convicted to dress modestly:

IT WAS AND WILL ALWAYS BE A HEART ISSUE; I'M NOW MORE SUBMISSIVE TO MY HUSBAND

"When I desired to understand the holiness of God, to fear the Lord and to separate from the world, my increased love for Him affected everything I did, even how I dressed. It was and will always be a heart issue.

"Years ago as a carnal Christian, I remember being uncomfortable around a woman in our former New Evangelical Church who consistently wore modest, long dresses. I was taught that those types of women were 'legalistic.' This teaching conveniently eased my being uncomfortable as I wore my jeans. I now realize I was under conviction. FALSELY LABELING A MODEST WOMAN LEGALISTIC EASES ONE'S CONSCIENCE FROM HOLY SPIRIT CONVICTION.

"As we began taking the Scriptures seriously and we started attending a fundamental church, the Lord led me to study modesty. I then began exchanging pants, sensual high heels, flashy jewelry and bold cosmetics for modest skirts and shoes as well as subtle jewelry and cosmetics.

"THIS WAS QUITE A PROCESS AS MY FLESH FOUGHT AGAINST BEING LOOKED DOWN AT BY THE WORLD AND THOSE WHO PROFESSED CHRIST. I no longer looked worldly and sensual, desiring to attract attention but rather modest, chaste and shamefaced. It also became more natural to purposely avoid filling the mind with

TV, magazines and catalogs with images of worldly, sensual models and actresses.

"The blessings of having my heart right in this area include being more loving and submissive to my husband. (Only he wears the pants in the family now.) The Lord has also now opened up opportunities for me to lead several young girls and a woman to the Lord as well as discipling other women.

"May women allow themselves to be led by God's word to bear the reproach and allow the Lord to bring conviction in our hearts where He desires. 'The fear of the LORD is the beginning of wisdom: and the knowledge of the holy is understanding' (Proverbs 9:10).

"I'm very grieved that while most women wear dresses and skirts to our fundamental church, not many wear them outside of church. I'm thankful we have two Pastors' wives who hold up the standard but most ignore this."

THE GODLY EXAMPLE OF PASTORS' WIVES AND THE WRITTEN STANDARDS WEREN'T ENOUGH

"Here is my testimony about how and why I came to have a Biblical conviction on modest clothing. ... We had been involved with an Independent Baptist church for about 1 1/2 years before I was saved at the age of 14. My Sunday School teacher was my godly Pastor's wife, who quickly became one of my heroes. She taught us well and I can remember her mentioning the way a lady should dress and why. Her life was a complete example of the way a Christian lady should act, walk, talk, dress, respect her husband and show Christ's love for all those around her. But it wasn't from her that I came to have a conviction about modest dress for myself. At 17-18 I attended an independent Baptist Bible college for one year. They had a very good dress code and I had no problem abiding by it thanks to the example and teaching of my Pastor's wife. But it wasn't there, either, that I was taught about why I needed to dress according to the dress code. At 25 my husband and I moved interstate so he could attend

Bible college as the Lord had called him to preach. At this college, again, I had a godly Pastor's wife whose life was also a complete example of a Christian woman. Here, though, I gained a better understanding of the subject as I attended my pastor's wife's college class. She did an excellent job in instructing us on how we should dress and why. ...

"My husband became a pastor and he believed in teaching the whole counsel of God -- which included modest apparel for women. ALTHOUGH I HAD BEEN TAUGHT THE SAME THING IT DIDN'T REALLY HIT HOME UNTIL I HEARD A MAN TEACH ON IT. I listened to my husband preach the Word of God and I gained understanding. It wasn't long before I came to understand more completely God's design for women and how He wants them to present themselves. I now have a Biblical conviction, thanks to a preacher who was doing his job. ...

"TODAY THIS SUBJECT IS NOT OFTEN PREACHED FROM THE PULPIT. THE PASTOR SAYS, 'I'LL LEAVE IT TO MY WIFE TO TEACH THE LADIES.' THE WIFE SAYS, 'I'LL JUST LIVE THE RIGHT WAY AND TEACH BY MY EXAMPLE.' IT DOESN'T WORK. IT DIDN'T WORK FOR ME AND SADLY IT ISN'T WORKING FOR THE MAJORITY OF YOUNG CHRISTIAN WOMEN IN CHURCHES TODAY. The Lord has blessed us with six children so far. We as parents have challenged them to study and seek God's mind on this subject, listen to the teaching they receive and pray for understanding and wisdom. We want them to have a Biblical conviction, not just, 'I'll do it because you do,' because that will not last."

[Note from Brother Cloud. The 200 e-mails I have received on this subject from men and women in many parts of the world bear out what this lady is saying. There are many churches that have a godly pastor's wife and some other women who are setting the example and even have some written dress standards, but the matter of truly modest dress isn't "trickling" down to girls and the younger women. A couple of pastors wrote to say that they do not believe this is a matter for the pulpit. I could not disagree more. It is, in fact, a matter that needs to be dealt with in a church from every direction in a kind and godly and patient and humble manner.]

MY CONVICTIONS ARE A SOURCE OF CONFLICT WITH MY FAMILY, BUT I DO NOT WANT TO GO BACK TO THE WAY I ONCE DRESSED

"I got saved out of a Catholic background. Dress standards were something I knew nothing about. My husband and his family had been attending independent Baptist churches for a few years (after coming out of Southern Baptist churches) but had never had any teaching about dress and consequently had no standards in that area. After we married, we began traveling a lot and attending other churches. We visited Bible Baptist Church in Elmont, New York, on our honeymoon and I was very interested to see that there were tracts in their rack entitled *Women in Pants*. I took one with me and read through it. I didn't make any changes because of it, but it planted the seed. About 2 years later, we visited Believers Baptist Church in Winona Lake, Indiana and were there for several days. It was my first real exposure to ladies who wore dresses all of the time. I began to think that maybe it WAS wrong to be wearing pants, but I still wasn't quite sure. Three months later, we were at a preaching conference at Independent Baptist Church in Ramsey, Minnesota. That was the final straw for me. Several of the preachers mentioned dress and I was finally convinced of the Biblical reasons for modesty. When I returned home from that trip I got rid of my pants and started replacing them with skirts and dresses. I even took sewing lessons so that I would be able to make modest clothing for my daughter and myself. Shortly thereafter, both of my sisters-in-law also became convicted about dressing modestly and got rid of their pants as well. My convictions about dress have been a source of contention between me and my family, but since I've come to believe that modesty is a Bible doctrine, I've never doubted it, nor have I ever wanted to go back to dressing the way I used to."

I FACED RIDICULE FROM MY FAMILY BUT MY HUSBAND SUPPORTED ME

"I was not raised in a Christian home. I was never exposed to godliness while I was growing up. I was saved by God's wonderful and amazing grace at the age of 28. After I got saved I had such a hunger to learn and to be different. I believe this hunger is God-given. ... I was already a new creature on the inside, but I had such a desire to be different on the outside although I didn't know what this would mean for me. God began working on me about the right way in the area of dress.

"It started with what I would wear to the House of God. You have to remember that I was not a church-goer before getting saved. So I didn't even own a dress or skirt. But I noticed that all the other ladies at church wore dresses. It wasn't long till God had a godly lady (our associate pastor's wife at the time) to befriend me and take me under her wing. Our children were close in age to one another and so we began spending much time together. When I went to her house the first few times I noticed she and her girls always had dresses or skirts on. ... I just naturally assumed that this was how a Christian lady was to dress. The thing with me, however, was my pride. I felt stupid asking her why they dressed that way. After all, how could it be wrong for a lady to wear pants when the lady that I worked with at the time who was instrumental in getting me in church and also in my getting saved wore pants?

"I began to pray and ask God to show me the truth in this thing of how I should dress. It took a few months of continuing to observe other ladies at church and wanting to know the truth in this thing before -- what do you think happened? -- our pastor preached about it. No, not an entire message about how we should dress, but he hit on it just enough for God to show me what I needed to do. He used Deuteronomy 22:5, 'The woman shall not wear that which pertaineth unto a man, neither shall a man put on a woman's garment: for all that do so are abomination unto the LORD thy God.' When we think of men we don't think of them as wearing a dress. We think of them as wearing pants. So pants pertains to a man.

"As God began to deal with me in the way I dressed I determined that if God wanted me to dress a certain way that He did not desire for me to dress a certain way at home and a different way for church. I had talked to my husband about what God was dealing with me about and he was very supportive and said that he didn't have a problem with me wanting to dress differently.

"I faced ridicule and persecution from family (which was the hardest to deal with), friends and even other brothers and sisters in Christ. I was accused of 'keeping up with the Joneses' since my associate pastor's wife who was having a great godly influence on me was a Jones. But I was determined to obey God no matter what. God blessed my obedience in this area of my life and began to deal with me in other areas of my life. There was such a peace in 'giving in' and surrendering to God in this area of my life. There was no longer the battle in my spirit that I had."

BY DRESSING DISTINCTIVELY I CAN BE A WITNESS EVEN WITHOUT TALKING

"I'm a fundamental Baptist Christian here in the Philippines. I have the conviction that as a Christian lady, I ought to be strictly following modest apparel for ladies and not to wear pants. Wearing modest apparel is one way of showing a difference in this wicked and crooked world. Through physical appearance, you can be identified as a Christian who strictly adheres to what the Bible teaches no matter what the world says to you. Since I was baptized and graduated from High School, I haven't worn pants at all, and it's really a great blessing to me. Even if not I'm saying anything or telling people that I'm a fundamental Baptist Christian, then the people around me know that I am because of the manner I am dressed. And when people start to question me about it, then I share my testimony and witness to them about the Gospel of Jesus Christ and how a person can be assured of Heaven when he dies. And I always thank the Lord for giving me a teachable heart."

A TESTIMONY FROM A 13-YEAR-OLD

"I am 13 years old and at a very young age my parents taught my sister and I, from God's Word, what the right way to dress really was. But I never came to a conviction myself until a while later. . . One day, about three years ago, I was on the shore of a lake with two young teenage girls (they were visiting with their grandparents who came to our church). It was a hot afternoon so they suggested we wade in the water. The younger girl, my sister and I pulled our skirts up to our knees (we all had long skirts on), and waded out into the water. The older girl stayed on shore and pulled her skirt off to reveal very short shorts. I was a little embarrassed. Then she said, 'Why don't you wear shorts?' I quickly answered, 'My parents said I can't; I don't know what's wrong with them.' Because I did not have my own Bible conviction I gave in very easily to peer pressure. My parents kept teaching us (and praying for us) about the way we should dress as a Christian. A short while after the above incident, Dad got me to do a study on 1 Timothy 2:9 to see what God says about how I should dress. The study made me think and after I had finished it I looked up other verses to see what they had to say about how I should dress as a Christian girl. As I began to find more verses and my parents kept teaching me I developed my own conviction on the way I believe God wants me to dress. It came through God's Word. From then on I have enjoyed wearing the clothes that my Father in heaven would approve. With mum's help I sew my own modest clothes. (We have to because there is nothing in the shops which is acceptable!) I am very thankful to my parents for teaching me the way they did and for encouraging me to study God's Word myself; otherwise I may never have come to my own Bible conviction on what modesty for women really is."

THE TESTIMONY OF AN ELEMENTARY CHRISTIAN SCHOOL PRINCIPAL

"I am a member of a fundamental Baptist church and elementary school principal of a Christian school. I never have felt comfortable in wearing pants, whether they were women's clothing or men's clothing. That was never the real issue of the reason I gave up wearing anything that looked like trousers. Anything that brought attention to certain parts of my body bothered me. My family made fun of me and even church people did, but I really wanted to know God, really know Him, and I did a study on His holiness. From that study many things happened and, of course, God spoke to me about my attire. In 1985, I was working in the football concession stand wearing women's jeans like all the other ladies and one of my senior Bible students saw me and said, 'Mrs. -------, you are wearing jeans!' I replied, "Well, ------, so is every other lady in this concession.' With astonishment he said, 'I guess I never thought that you would.' It threw me back so much, that from that day on, I never wore them in public again. When my husband and I would go to the woods camping and hunting, I would wear them, but after a while, I thought, 'It is not worth offending anyone, especially God's people!' So, therefore, I gave up pants and anything that looked like them. ... My first year as coach at the school was difficult as I took the girls out of shorts and pants and had special culottes made. They rebelled and I had to deal with moms more than the girls, but we all got through it and amazingly had a wonderful year! The girls went soul-winning

175

with me and we became very close that season. We won the state championship in volleyball that year, and to this day, the girls bring up that 'special' season where they grew so much in the Lord. The battle is tough for us women, but it is worth it. It's funny, but rock music in the church and women in pants in the church are sensitive areas for many women. We have had families leave our church because the 'moms' get turned inside out over music and teen's attire--mostly our young ladies' pants. If women would just listen to the Holy Spirit, there would be no decision to make; it is already decided. To me, now in my 60's, to have made that decision has been far more rewarding than to have had my own way."

I AM CONSIDERED OLD FASHIONED AND I LOVE EVERY MINUTE OF IT

"I got saved in a Baptist church eight years ago wearing very immodest dress. The next day, though no one told me to go out and dress modest (so I credit it to the Holy Spirit), I went to Wal-Mart and bought a modest loose-fitting, floor-length church dress (which they don't carry anymore). ... I also had a few long denim jumpers and wore the same things over and over. I met my husband there and we married a year later. He had been saved there two years earlier and had been praying for a wife. I asked him why he chose me because there were so many young girls in the church. He said he wanted a modest girl who loved the Lord. The other girls were not, and outside of church they were rebellious.

"My husband received orders to Korea a short time later and I was home alone for a year. I was faithful to church but didn't notice that I was conforming to the dress styles of the other ladies and girls in the church. In the meantime, my husband attended a strong fundamental Baptist church run by a missionary, which preached the KJV and standards. When returning from Korea, my husband didn't agree with my tight clothing and capris, etc. Our church didn't preach standards and in the time we had been there, every teen that graduated never came back and lived rebellious lives; the pastor's best friend, a deacon in the church, was having an open affair, etc.

"My husband said it was time to find a different church where the entire Bible was preached. So now we went to a different church and our pastor preached standards and I was immediately convicted and changed my dress styles. All my old friends called me legalistic and stop talking to me. Even in our church now, I have seen a big change in dress styles. The teenagers wear the skirts that come to the knee but when they bend over or sit down...well you know. Their tops are low cut with a v and look like they were painted on. ... My husband leads the music and he said he can't even look at the people because there are so many short skirts etc.

"I learned how to sew a few years ago. The Lord has allowed me to make my seven-year-old daughter's clothes, which are modest dresses and very full and old fashioned. What surprises me is that wherever we go, people stop us and say how beautiful my daughter looks in such pretty dresses, but they dress their daughters (even three and four year olds) in tight immodest clothing. I have had to start making my own dresses also, because the department stores are pricy and it is getting harder and harder to find modest clothing.

"I also have to tell you this. A few years back, we had a few new couples join the church. The two ladies wore short skirts and tight low tops. It didn't take long and some of our teenage girls from church started dressing that way. Now, pretty much most of them dress that way. And one mother recently told me that she allowed her daughter to dress that way because her daughter felt singled out and not liked. ... Then another lady told me that she allows her daughters to dress that way because 'you have to let them pick their own style or they will grow up to hate the Lord and have nothing to do with church.'

"There is one particular preacher in our church that preaches hard on standards and some won't even be there when he preaches because they say he is not preaching the Bible and he hurts their feelings and he is a dictator.

"I always ask my husband's opinion on every thing I wear. Because even sometimes I may have something on that he says is too tight in the back or front. ... I'm not perfect, not even close, but I see the younger ladies (and by the way I am only 28) dressing on the edge and even over the edge and the younger girls are using them as an excuse to dress the same way.

"I am considered old fashioned and I love every minute of it.

"I just don't understand because my pastor preaches standards and my pastor's wife sets the best example of dress, but so many professing Christian ladies don't dress that way anymore. I am thankful that I am saved and my husband loves me and the Lord loves me."

TESTIMONY OF A 17-YEAR-OLD MISSIONARY KID

"I am a 17-year-old missionary daughter. At first my conviction of not wearing pants did not come on my own. When I was in 3rd grade I was not allowed to wear pants anymore. (My parents got convicted about it.) I'm a stubborn willed person and when I was 13 I started getting an attitude on what I had to wear. Thankfully my parents were just as stubborn for the Lord. After much preaching and teaching and good examples around me the Lord convicted me that I should be modest and please him.

"Keep in mind that was with a godly Christian home, strong preaching, and good examples all around me. And yet it was still hard for me to remove my foot from evil. Now imagine how hard it is for those Christian teen girls trying to please the Lord in an ungodly environment. Hardly any preaching, lots of bad examples, and made fun of when they try to do what is right.

"It does not get much harder than in the modern Latin culture. Here I teach a teenage girl's class with newly saved girls from horrific backgrounds. I can now see the problems over and over. … Just when I thought I was failing in teaching them, the Lord sends encouragement. One girl comes up to me and says, 'Thank you. I've been watching you. The way you dress, act, talk. How do you do it with all the peer pressure?' Talk about humbling. It gave a wonderful opportunity to brag about the Lord. I told her it's not my own strength, nor is it me, because if I tried on my own I would fail for sure every time! But when the Lord convicts us and we surrender our stubborn wills to what he wants, you will be amazed what He can do with a sinner saved by grace. Ever since I have seen her try to dress, act and talk right. In college here they chide her, but I tell her she may be the only Bible some of them ever read. She gives out tracts and Bibles to classmates.

"Pants only attract the wrong attention and the only way to change your attitude is surrender, to desire to please the LORD more than yourself and the world."

I WORE DRESSES TO CHURCH, BUT I DID NOT WANT TO GIVE UP MY PANTS; THEY WERE COMFORTABLE

"My husband and I both were raised in Christian homes. When we married we moved to Ohio, and attended a Bible church for 18 years. God moved us out of that church two years ago this June. We had boys in the teen department at that time. The girls dressed in very skimpy clothing, some of it was so bad it would embarrass me. The music was contemporary and rock. The youth director at that time loved the rock music and did not care to discuss any thing with us. So we ended up getting mocked for our stand. I couldn't believe how we were treated. We knew God was moving us out of that church.…

"I rarely ever saw teen girls wearing dresses; they would always wear tight jeans. One thing my husband and I noticed was that he had led a friend to the Lord and he and his wife started attending church with us. They started out dressing in nice clothes; she wore dresses. It wasn't long before she started wearing her pants. I thought this was sad that she had been wrongly influenced by the crowd at church. A good part of all the women wear pants on a regular basis to the services. I saw a worker once in the Masters Club wearing short shorts. It is sad.

"We moved on to another church in a town close by. We were only there for one year. I didn't think the clothing could be worse but over time we realized it was. The music was a little better. I had to talk to the assistant pastor about my eight-year-old daughter's teacher wearing a mini skirt to class with her legs hanging out, tattoo and all. Once again we were ridiculed for our stand. He told me her heart was right. The pastor spoke about it from the pulpit, how I shouldn't have said anything about it. But the pastor's daughter wore tight jeans and shirts, so how could he say anything.

"The Lord led us to a small church in the same town. What a difference!! The pastor's wife and several of the women wear dresses all the time. I had always worn dresses to church. My mother always wore dresses all the time as well as many of my aunts when I was growing up. They eventually started wearing pants. My two godly grandmothers always wore dresses; I never saw either one in a pair of pants. My husband started talking to me about me and our daughter wearing dresses all the time. I will be honest with you and say that I wasn't taking this too well. I wore dresses to church, but I did not want to give up my pants; they were comfortable. Through my husband's prayer, studying God's Word, and testimonies of women from my church I started getting convicted about it. Our pastor's wife had her sister come and speak at a ladies meeting. She talked about pleasing the Lord. She said someone had questioned her about

180

wearing dresses all the time and she said she believed it was pleasing to the Lord for her to dress modestly and dress like a lady.

"I have a daughter that I have to be an example to. Little by little we are still growing. My daughter and I started wearing dresses just last November. I've been laughed at by other Christians and have had a lot of things said to me. But I know I am doing what is pleasing to the Lord. I'm thankful for my husband being so patient with me; that was a help. Also being in a church where the people are trying to live separated lives is a help. … I know women in the world dress like harlots. And you can't get away from it when you go to the stores, but I don't expect my husband and teenage sons to be exposed to all the nudity in the church."

I DECIDED TO GIVE IN AND LET GOD HANDLE IT

"I was saved in 1978. For about 12 years I still wore pants and shorts. We changed churches and our pastor's family held high standards. For about five years I watched my preacher's wife with much admiration. God starting convicting me about pants, shorts, and swimwear. One day I just decided to give in and let God handle it. I have never looked back. Sometimes when we are out I am the only woman in a dress or skirt. I get looks all the time but it doesn't bother me. It's been about 17 years now and some members of my family still don't understand. But God is more important."

BEFORE I WAS SAVED I WORE CLOTHES TO SHOW OFF "MY BETTER ATTRIBUTES"

"I did not get saved until I was forty. Before I accepted Jesus, I wouldn't think twice about wearing something tight or short in order to 'show off' some of my better attributes. I didn't dress like a slut by any means, but I felt it was fine to wear shorts and T-shirts around town. After my conversion I started attending a liberal Presbyterian church. After less than a year, I found myself led by what I now know to be the Holy Spirit to a fundamental Independent Baptist church. The first time I walked in I noticed that all the women wore dresses or skirts, and there I was in my nice slacks and blouse. The members were very friendly and no one said a word to me, but God laid it upon my heart that I needed to wear skirts, so I did.

"And as the weeks went by, I found myself wearing my jeans and pants less and less, until I gave them up, of my own free will, because I knew that I wanted to wear 'modest' clothing, not because of any pressure from anyone. About that time I also started letting my hair grow longer. It is now halfway down my back, and still growing. I decided not to cut my hair after reading about how a woman's long hair is a glory to her, and is her covering. The word of God just convicted me that I needed to let it grow, again, to be modest."

I DON'T WANT TO BE A STUMBLING BLOCK TO ANYONE, NOR DO I WANT TO DRAW ATTENTION TO ANYTHING OTHER THAN MY FACE

"My conviction about not wearing pants came about gradually. When I was a young Christian in my twenties, I thought nothing of wearing pants. Having been a worldly, immodestly dressed teenager from a non-Christian home during the sixties and seventies, I graduated to wearing what I considered very modest, conservative clothes, such as a blouse tucked into form-fitting jeans. On Sundays, I wore a dress to church, because I felt I should look my best for God, but on Wednesdays, I wore jeans to church. At the time, I thought I was a very modest, conservative dresser--especially compared to other women I knew. One Wednesday night while I was standing, singing in the congregation, a question popped into my mind: 'Why do you want to look your best for God on Sundays, but not on Wednesdays?' Why was 'meeting with God on a Wednesday' any different from 'meeting with Him on a Sunday?' I couldn't answer that question, and the inconsistency bothered me so much that I stopped wearing pants to church on Wednesdays.

"Our family often sat around in the living room during the evenings having spiritual discussions. That's where we became convicted about many things, such as music and dress. When our oldest son came home from his first year at college (Ambassador Baptist College), we started questioning whether or not it was immodest to wear a bathing suit. We lived on the New Jersey shore where my husband and I were born and raised. We grew up on the beach and never thought a thing about wearing a bathing suit. I would have said that it was 'appropriate attire for the beach.' Well, after an entire evening of batting this around, we all came to the conclusion that even the most modest bathing suit was immodest. I PICTURED MYSELF WALKING DOWN THE AISLE OF OUR CHURCH ON A SUNDAY MORNING WEARING NOTHING BUT HIGH HEELS AND A BATHING SUIT, AND IT WAS A SHOCKING THOUGHT. IF IT WAS TOO IMMODEST FOR CHURCH, THEN IT WAS TOO IMMODEST FOR THE BEACH! That was the end of bathing suits for us!

"After that, I became more and more sensitive to the topic of modesty. I read many books and articles on the subject, in addition to studying what God said about it in the Bible. I started meditating on the word 'shamefacedness' in 1 Timothy 2:9. I read Isaiah 47:1-3 which opened my eyes to what God thinks about showing the thigh. As I was doing this, I was wearing skirts more, wearing pants less, and feeling much more feminine.

"My husband and I also spent many hours discussing the subject of women's pants, trying to decipher whether or not they were modest. He was leaning toward the view that pants were NOT modest, but I could not understand how loose-fitting slacks fit into that category. My grandmother had worn loose-fitting pink or powder blue polyester pant suits, and she looked very modest to me! My husband told me that in his opinion, MOST women's pants are immodest, because they are form-fitting and show the woman's shape, especially the derriere. This, he said, is appealing to men, and it causes them to lust. At first, I just could not believe this. Not being a man, I don't know how men think. But my husband was very strong about this, as if he really KNEW that most men think this way. By faith, I took my husband's word for it, figuring that he knew better than I, what appeals to men. After that, I read different publications and even listened to tapes that attested to what my husband had said. THIS IS PROBABLY THE MAIN THING THAT CONVINCED ME THAT MOST WOMEN'S PANTS ARE IMMODEST---THE KNOWLEDGE OF WHAT MEN ARE THINKING WHEN THEY SEE A WOMAN IN PANTS. I was convicted by this, because even though I may not think I look attractive in pants, a man might think so, and that is enough reason not to wear them. I don't want to be a stumbling block to anyone, nor do I want to draw attention to anything other than my face.

"I haven't worn pants for several years now, and it has actually been easier than having to decide whether or not a particular pair of pants is modest. It has been a freedom knowing that I'm modestly dressed, that I'm not causing men to lust, and that I'm pleasing God."

I WAS CONVICTED BY THE CULTURAL DEATH OF THE MODEST AND FEMININE WOMAN

"My husband and I attend a fundamental Baptist church in Ohio. Several months before we began attending our church the Father got my attention through a picture at a Railroad Museum. I remember seeing the picture hanging on the wall and it depicted a generation many decades ago. The women were dressed very modest and distinctly female. The men, likewise, were very nicely dressed and appeared distinctly male.

"Not too long after that my husband was in the hospital and we watched a documentary on the Toledo Zoo. We don't watch television so this was something out of the ordinary for us. As we watched the documentary about the zoo and the changes over the years. I noticed how women had changed in their attire. Over the decades as the zoo progressed in growth you saw the women and how in early years as zoo attenders the females were, again, distinctly female. As the years progressed, in the documentary of the zoo, you could see the women becoming less feminine and modest, and actually blending in and looking more like the males. It was such a vivid picture of the death of the modest and feminine woman.

"I believed the Father was telling me to be a feminine and modest woman in my dress and attire. It was life changing."

HOW HORRIBLE IF I HAD PERSISTED IN MY OWN WAY AND LED MY GIRLS INTO REBELLION IN THIS AREA

"I grew up in a strong Christian home, a Pastor's home, with biblical standards. However, after I was married I wore pants briefly. I knew it was wrong, and after about six months under conviction I returned to skirts and dresses; but I still dressed to please myself. You will hear over and over that dress reveals the heart and that is absolutely true. There are only two options here: you will dress to please God or you will dress to please yourself. Over the years, as I have come to the place where I just want God and His will, I have surrendered this area of my life to Him. Now I believe my skirts and dresses truly glorify Him, not myself. Our two daughters, ages 11 & 13, are being guided by my example. How horrible if I had persisted in my own way, and led them into rebellion in this area. I was thrilled recently to be able to do a Bible study with some young Christian women on the subject of modesty and dress! That God would allow me to do so is a wonderful picture of His grace! I would challenge you to consider the Biblical principles of Separation from the World, Gender Distinction, and Modesty for yourself. 1 Corinthians 6:19, 20 spoke to me in this area. God says we are bought, we are not our own, so glorify God in your BODY and in your spirit -- both are His."

I WAS A NEW AGER

"Before becoming an independent fundamental Baptist I was a New Ager. I was a Tomboy growing up and wore jeans and T shirt as a teenager. Before Salvation, I would attend Pentecostal churches upon occasion but ALWAYS wore a dress or skirt, of modest length. I liked it. I have read some good arguments against pants, the best of which is that they certainly aren't modest. They show one's private lines in the crotch area, hardly modest. They also show one's hip lines, also not modest. We still cannot get this across to our members, many of which wear jeans and just don't understand that their shape is well evident, especially from the back. These are not young, slight teens, these are overweight adult women with three or more children under their belt, so to speak, and I look no better than they, but I sure wouldn't willingly embarrass myself by forcing people to look at it. A nice, long, flouncy dress hides this nicely.

"The one argument I hate is that "I just want to be comfortable!' As tight as some of those pants are, how can they be comfortable? I hate having a wad of double-sewn jean fabric cutting me there; how comfortable is that? Dresses are easy for me, far more comfortable, and in the winter, extra shielding against the cold. Lest they think we need run around bare legged underneath, there are any number of leggings and warmies that go nicely, and the one or two loose flouncy skirts on the outside are that much more protection to me in freezing cold winds which we get a lot of. The skirts just cut the wind chill. I often wear the leggings all the way to the ankle covered with a boot and no one ever sees the leggings.

"I have my farm dresses, wonderful, comfortable tough denim, with big pockets to carry my carrots and vitamin C (chewable) for the goats, or eggs from the chicken house, or tools, or screws and nails, or hoof trimming tools. Can't beat them.

"Of course some of my ideas about self sufficiency are lost on the other IFB's, I'm shocked how many don't know how to cook. Or sew, let alone all the crafty things I grew up learning as normal (embroidery, sewing, quilting, having animals to raise your own food, easy things like chickens, rabbits). And I had hobbies I learned out of books. Leather braiding bridles for ponies, basketry, and many women's crafts like knitting and crochet. These things are becoming lost arts. As a 20 something, I learned how to clean wool, spin wool and weave wool. Now I have my own sheep. I milk my own goats."

I ALMOST SAID, "I WON'T WEAR DRESSES ALL THE TIME FOR YOU OR GOD!"

"I was not raised in a Christian home. ... During the summer I typically wore very short cut off shorts, sleeveless shirts, and always skimpy bathing suits. Is it any wonder I had a baby when I was 17? When my daughter was three years old I got saved. When my daughter was five I got married. We attended a very charismatic southern Baptist church. It wasn't uncommon for people to come to church looking like they just got out of bed. I wore my cut off blue jean shorts on more than one occasion. My motto was if you can wear it on Monday, you can wear it on Sunday! Through a series of providential events, and a lot of late night study on my husband's part, we left the church in search of a KJV Independent Baptist church. As I grew in the Lord, I began to dress more modestly. My shorts grew longer until they turned into pants. (Eventually my pants turned into skirts!) I had come a LONG way.

"When we went to the new church, the pastor came and talked to us, he said that I and my daughter would be expected to wear dresses to church. That bugged me, but I complied. ... The general thinking is if I can get them to dress right on Sunday, I have accomplished something. What you accomplish is creating or at least aiding hypocrisy in this area. I still felt that what I wear each day should be appropriate for church, but since I had agreed when we joined the church I just submitted.

"My husband began 'dropping hints' that modest dress was more than we thought. I agreed, women should dress modestly, and I was dressing modestly, I thought. He gradually got around to telling me that he was beginning to think women should wear skirts or dresses all the time. I felt my blood beginning to boil. The more he studied the more I was annoyed. Of course he would study something that applied to me not him, I thought! I had never before thought he was wrong, and we went from being in a charismatic southern Baptist church, to a very conservative independent Baptist church, and I had always been proud of his studying and teaching our family. Never before had I thought him to be wrong. He didn't harp on it, but he did mention it from time to time. At one point he brought it up and I became so annoyed with the subject that I almost said, 'I won't wear dresses all the time for you or God!' That thought scared me. Though I didn't actually speak it aloud, the thought did come out of the abundance of my heart. I began wearing dresses, but only to please my husband. It was not my conviction; I thought I knew more than him. I thought he was coming to this conclusion because he was getting independent preacher friends, and it was just the thing to do. I had a long, hard, bitter struggle.

"Some of the reasons I came up with were: 1. I can't do everything I need to do in a skirt. 2. It is man's tradition being passed off as the Word of God, and Jesus let the Pharisees have it for that very thing. 3. It is not practical in the winter. 4. If pants are form fitting, and men are attracted to them, then my not wearing them will cause my husband to be attracted to other women and not me. 5. It will kill my ability to witness to people because they will think I am weird. 6. If you can wear it on Monday you can wear it on Sunday!

"Eventually God broke through my hard heart and gave me answers to all of my objections. He also showed me how shallow they were! I can do what I need to do in a skirt; I can even ride a bike and mow the lawn. I couldn't, however, do those things in a tight business-type skirt. A skirt that allows freedom is very long, loose and flowing! When I purchase skirts, if the skirt stops me from taking a full step, I don't buy it. It may be modest, but it will be annoying when chasing a child through the yard! Skirts are much cooler in the summer, and if a skirt is long and loose and you wear a pair of long johns underneath it is quite warm. A godly husband will always be attracted to modest femininity. I came to realize that how we dress is a part of our witness, and we don't have to look like the world to witness to the world. We are a better witness if we don't look like the world.

"At least one thing I have always believed is true. If you can wear it on Monday, you can wear it on Sunday. Sometimes you just have to be willing to change what you are wearing on Monday. God's ways are always best. Modesty and femininity are freedom, not bondage as I had always thought."

Survey of Men on the Subject of Women's Dress

I sent out a notice to the Fundamental Baptist Information Service e-mail list and asked the following question of the men on the list who are members of fundamentalist and independent Baptist churches:

"In your opinion, which of the following items of female dress cause a real potential for lust?"

- short skirts
- tight skirts
- slit skirts
- long skirts with slits to the knees
- sleeveless blouses
- low cut blouses and dresses
- tight blouses
- sheer blouses
- T-shirts
- V-neck dresses
- form-fitting jeans
- looser-fitting pants
- shorts
- one piece bathing suits

[We included peddle pushers and capris in the original survey but most of the men did not know what they are, so it turned out that the comments on those items were too irrelevant to include in this book.]

My objective in this is to help girls and women in strong Bible-believing churches to understand how men think, not only men in the world or men in churches in general but men in the very churches that they attend.

I received a flood of response to this survey. In just one day I received well over 100 responses from men ages 24 to 74 and from many parts of the world, and that was on a weekend, and they are still coming in a week and a half later. This tells me that there is a readiness on the part of men to let women understand how they see this issue.

As you will see, the responses were very earnest. The men are discouraged that lust is such a powerful temptation in their lives, and they admitted that it is so. Some of the men literally begged me to tell the women that their manner of dress is important and that they need to understand how men look at things.

One man wrote: "Thank for this request. This area is the greatest challenge in my life -- in all honesty to a brother-in-the-Blood."

The following was also typical:

> "I have been saved for about eight years and the lust issue is huge for me and for all men. ... I need God every day to help me stay away from lust. Short Skirts, tight blouses, slit dresses are all over. You can't look at billboards, grocery store waiting line magazine racks, Internet advertisements, walking in the park, or any store. You get my point; it's everywhere. ... I have to pray everyday for God to keep lust out of my way. I wish I was born into a good Bible believing church and was brought up to stay away from lustful sin. To answer your question it would have to be anything short or tight on a woman. I look forward to the cold winters up north when women cover everything up."

Another man said:

> "That our society drenches every inch of media in sexually explicit advertising is a source of much temptation, sadness and concern for this man. Facing that sort of issue with Christian sisters in a church setting is most grievous."

Most of the men observed that their response to a woman's immodest dress depends on their spiritual condition and acknowledged that they have a responsibility before God not to lust after women regardless of how they are dressed.

For example, one man said: "Men are sight oriented creatures. The Lord has so equipped men to be sexually stimulated visually. ... Men must govern their own hearts."

Another man said: "My response to immodesty is often dependent on the environment, situation and my spiritual defense mechanism at a particular moment. If I have had a wonderful prayer time and clothed myself with all the spiritual armor, I am usually just about OK for anything. But more often then I would like it, I am not prepared or I am in a vulnerable situation; then I better run for my dear life (Gen. 39:12)."

Another man said: "While I feel that the Lord has helped me overcome in this area [of not lusting after women], the enemy knows my weakness and still attacks me. In my opinion, the key to overcoming lust are: 1) Obey God's Word, especially the command to abstain from the very appearance of evil; and 2) don't put yourself in situations where you will encounter women scantily dressed (i.e. the beach, certain television programs, etc.). Since we are in the world, I know that there is no way to completely avoid the things that tempt us, but if we will stay true to the Word of God and allow Him to help us, we can be 'more than conquerors through Him who loved us' (Romans 8:37)."

Many of the men also observed that this is a heart issue. The following statement by a pastor is typical of those made by many others:

> "I believe the most important issue in female modesty is the issue of a chaste heart. If the woman desires to please her Saviour and honor her brother in Christ, there is seldom an issue with the clothing she wears. Mandating modest clothing without focusing on creating a chaste heart does little good. If the woman wears 'modest' clothing but is sensual in the way she walks or conducts herself, it will invariably cause a man to lust. I don't need

to see skin to cause me to lust. We men have pretty good imaginations."

As to the individual items of dress, the men made the following points:

First of all, many of the men replied that *all* of the aforementioned female dress styles hold a real potential for lust. The following two statements were typical:

"I believe that ALL you had listed cause a 'potential' for lust."

"I think that ALL of the listed items can cause lust. The bottom line for me is that anything that is form fitting, exposing, sheer, or clinging to a woman is immodest and can cause men to lust."

Comments on the specific items of apparel fell along the following lines:

SHORT SKIRTS AND SHORT DRESSES AND SHORTS hold a very serious potential for lust for men. One man said, "The higher up on a woman's leg, the more lustful/tempting it becomes."

TIGHT CLOTHING is at least as much of a potential problem for men as skimpy clothing. Most of the men indicated that **TIGHT SKIRTS AND TIGHT BLOUSES AND FORM-FITTING JEANS AND ONE-PIECE BATHING SUITS** hold a "VERY great potential" for lust. One man said tight skirts are "very inviting and a potential for lust." Another said of tight clothing, "You don't even need to see skin; they provide all the curves." Another said: "I would say the number one problem is any garment that is form fitting, be it jeans, pants, skirt, dress, shirt, whatever. Anything that is tight, no matter how long it is, leaves nothing to the imagination, and that defeats the whole purpose of covering the skin in the first place!" Another said: "One thing I see in my church is tight clothing. Oh, it may very well be covering but it is revealing the shape in a woman. This can be even more tantalizing to a man."

Another wrote: "The point is that it is not the type of clothing that can trip a man up, rather it is the amount and the level of cling to the body." One man said that since one-piece bathing suits are "skin tight" he does "not think any red blooded normal man could look purely on a woman attired like this." Some of the men also mentioned **LOW-RIDING JEANS** as a cause for serious concern, because not only do they totally emphasize the woman's figure but they are also suggestive of a bare midriff even if covered with a T-shirt. The T-shirt in such a case is invariably tight, of course.

SLIT SKIRTS AND SLIT DRESSES are a problem for many men. One man answered the question of whether slit skirts are a real potential for lust with the reply, "Oh! Yes." One man said that slit skirts "tempt your imagination." Another called the slit skirt the "peek-a-boo" skirt, while another said the slit is "designed to catch the eye." A pastor said, "They are a teasing game, catching the attention of a guy's eyes with the promise of more; it is an enticement to sin." One man said: "My belief is that any slit (whether it be a long, medium, or short skirt) provides a flash of skin that is enticing to the eye and the flesh of men. It is the 'forbidden fruit,' so to speak, that is covered and when the woman sits or moves just right, that part of the leg is exposed and it is all a man needs to think about what he just saw or what else he could see." Another man said: "I know that many women cannot begin to understand how that a skirt or dress that is 2 inches off the floor in length, but has a long slit anywhere on it, front, back or side, can cause a man to lust. They think that we are pathetic, and unfortunately I have to agree." Another man said: "For me personally, slits draw my eyes where they shouldn't be drawn. If anyone knows anything about advertising, he would know that advertisers use lines to draw people's eyes where they want (company logo, name, whatever). Slits in skirts do exactly the same thing." Another observed, "If the slit is there because the dress or skirt is too tight, why not wear a loose skirt?" Some men said that the slits are not a problem if they are not above the knee.

SHEER BLOUSES OR DRESSES are a problem for the vast majority of men. One man said, "I see a lot of Christian women wearing sun dresses in the summer because they are cool. They are also revealing and alluring. Most summer clothes are thin so as to be more comfortable. But you let that woman wearing these clothes stand with a light source behind her (such as the sun) and there is nothing left to the imagination. You can see her form in every detail and it will get men frothing at the mouth, lusting after that woman. Is it the man's fault for not controlling his flesh and desires even though it is there for him to see? Absolutely! But it is equally the woman's fault for not having enough godliness about her to dress modestly in the first place."

Even **LOOSER-FITTING FEMALE PANTS**, while not as much of a problem as form-fitting jeans, hold a potential problem for many men. One man said, "While it is true that some things on your list will draw your attention quicker and cause you to look longer, even 'looser-fitting pants' direct a man's gaze to the area of the hips." Another wrote: "A few years ago, I preached a message about standards (including music, dress, and others). I asked for a show of hands as to how many men would admit their eyes were drawn to a woman's crotch when she wore pants instead of a skirt or dress. More than two dozen hands went up (and who knows how many more were hesitant to make the public confession with their wives right next to them?). The group included many of the finest Christians I know, some of whom are ordained ministers and missionaries." Many men mentioned the unisex aspect of looser pants on women.

As for **V-NECK DRESSES**, most men said they are not a problem as long as the V is shallow. A few said the V-neck itself, even if not too low, can be a problem because it acts like an arrow pointing to a place where their eyes should not roam.

As for **SLEEVELESS BLOUSES**, many of the men mentioned that they can be a problem because they can allow a man to see something he should not see and "the potential for peeking is there." A pastor commented, "There is too much of an opportunity for parts of a woman's anatomy to inadvertently show through to the public that are only to be revealed to her husband in private." One man said: "One word about sleeveless dresses or tops. When the woman has her arm raised or in a certain position, the sleeve hole will open in just a way that you can see inside her shirt and see the woman's underwear or even more. No woman, much less a Christian woman, should ever wear clothing that reveals her body!"

When it comes to **T-SHIRTS** on females, the men said they are not a problem unless they are tight or expose the midriff or you can see through them or they have writings/logos/pictures at the breast level. One pastor said: "It depends on the fit, cut, thickness of the material and color. A modest T-shirt would be loose fitting, non-see-through, of a thick enough material to truly be modest. Unfortunately very few T-shirts fit these qualifications." One man said: "My wife sews attractive vests that she and our daughter wear over T-shirts. It's a way of using clever camouflage to be modest." One woman mentioned another problem with T-shirts: "I have a problem with smart-alecky T-shirts. I have a hard time finding T-shirts for my daughter sometimes, not so much from a tightness standpoint, but they have inappropriate sayings on them that encourage a worldly attitude, rebellion against parents, etc." A man wrote along similar lines in regard to "Christian T-shirts," warning about "Jesus T-shirts like 'This Blood's For You,' etc., that really degrade the message of Scripture."

CONSIDER SOME EXCERPTS FROM THE
COMMENTS MADE BY THE MEN:

"I do believe most women just do not know how men think. Period. I believe that there is a whole segment, group, class of women, who, if they really understood men, would change their dress code, because they do want to please God. Not all women, by far, but some would. *They just need to understand it's not just a list of do's and don'ts set forth to force them in to 'frumpiness,' but a desire of godly men to gain their cooperation in helping them NOT lust, and to not be stumbling blocks, because they just want to please God.*"

"MANY WOMEN, USUALLY YOUNGER, DRESS TO ATTRACT MEN AND DO NOT KNOW HOW DANGEROUS IT TRULY CAN BE FOR THEM. ... I am a retired criminal investigator and worked criminal work for 17 1/2 years of my career. I think many homicides and serious physical assaults in addition to the obvious sex crimes are brought about by immodest dress and any born again Christian woman should never dress as such. A sexual predator can be turned on and be as dangerous as a hand grenade with the pin pulled by a women that has the one turn on factor for his mind (which is a variable with such criminals) which could be any of the listed ways of dressing."

"I am glad you are addressing this issue. This issue along with worldly music has come into fundamental churches like a tidal wave. Thank you for being a watchman!"

"I have to admit some of the dresses that are worn even though the dress hits the floor, and some of the blouses, even though it goes all the way to the neck, are very form fitting. I don't think that women are out to stumble the men of the church, and nor am I saying that women need to walk around in sacks. There are sometimes when a lady is doing a special music or something that I have to look away that I may not stumble. In summation I think that all of the clothing you have listed that is form fitting and shows the curves of a woman is a real potential for lust."

"I am a 24-year-old, unmarried man. I am very glad that you are asking us men about this issue, because it has been my experience that women truly do not understand the things that can run through a man's head when he sees an immodestly-dressed woman. For a God-fearing man, this is a true concern. Fashionable clothing is not, as far as I can tell, designed by God-fearing Christians with any interest in modesty. Sex sells, and sexy clothing sells. ... I have talked to women I know about the dress issue and told them that when they wear certain things, no matter how 'covered up' they may be, the fit of the clothing still makes a huge difference. Some women have told me that it is a man's fault for having such a dirty mind or for letting it get to a point where lust becomes a problem, but the fact is men seem specifically prone to these types of thoughts. In North American culture we are inundated with sex. Everywhere we look there is a provocatively dressed (or practically undressed) woman selling something, and I think that women (and men) need to seriously consider the way they dress and how it affects members of the opposite sex. The last place I want to have to worry about lust is in my church. AS CHRISTIANS, IT IS NOT OUR PLACE TO SAY, 'WELL, I JUST DON'T UNDERSTAND WHY MEN CAN'T LOOK AT ME DRESSED LIKE THIS AND NOT BATTLE WITH LUSTING THOUGHTS.' INSTEAD, WE NEED TO TAKE IT FOR TRUTH WHEN A PERSON OF THE OPPOSITE SEX INFORMS US THAT OUR DRESS IS CAUSING PROBLEMS FOR THEM, AND DO WHAT WE NEED TO DO TO PROTECT OUR BROTHERS AND SISTERS FROM STUMBLING."

"I am 64 years old now and walking with the Lord Jesus through life. Earlier in my life I was a womanizer as a single man for a long time. MY FEELINGS OF WOMEN DRESSING IMMODESTLY ARE STRONG, AS I KNOW THE SADNESS THAT INFIDELITY, LUSTFUL SIN AND ADULTERY BRING ABOUT TO MANY, AND

IMMODEST DRESS IS A PRECURSOR TO THE AFOREMENTIONED ACTIVITIES."

"All men are aroused in one way or the other over revealed flesh. That is exactly why these clothes are made this way. I know some men are more easily aroused than others but normally any man is naturally inclined (by our sinful nature) to take notice of a woman wearing any garment that is revealing flesh. I THINK IT IS A SHAME TO COME TO CHURCH AFTER A WEEK IN THIS EVIL WORLD AND WANT TO ENJOY A SERVICE OF WORSHIP AND PRAISE TO THE LORD AND FELLOWSHIP AMONG SEPARATED PEOPLE AND SEE WOMEN DRESSING LIKE THE WORLD AND WHEN YOU CONFRONT THEM ABOUT THIS YOU ALWAYS GET THE SAME OLD LINE 'WELL IF YOU DON'T LIKE IT, YOU'VE GOT THE PROBLEM.' Well, I always wonder why a woman who loves the Lord and wants to please the Lord would want to dress like the world and have men looking at her in a carnal way. When I see a woman in a store in town and she is dressed a certain conservative way, I always think, 'I bet she is a Christian.' IT SAYS A LOT ABOUT THE CHARACTER OF A WOMAN WHEN SHE SHUNS THE STYLES OF THIS WORLD AND WALKS IN SUCH A WAY THAT SHE WANTS TO LET PEOPLE KNOW THAT SHE IS DIFFERENT."

"One of the sad things I observe in church is the control that the fashion world has over women and the lack of communication between man and wife. I have been saved for 45 years come August and have been in an independent Baptist Church for 40 years. ... I see women and teenagers in our church and have to look away or up so as not to be seen looking at how they are dressed. Modesty seems to be an archaic word to many and it grieves me."

"I am 55 years old and I am BROKENHEARTED over the dress of a great number of females in the churches I visit. Oh, if I could only talk to moms and dads. I have never been married but lived in the world many years. I beg you, preacher, tell them that wearing ANYTHING that draws attention to a particular area, accentuating ANY form or flesh, is a great distraction for me. Please, stop wearing TIGHT clothing, exposing flesh, and wearing articles of clothing with writing on them. How many times have I had to turn my eyes away, or worry, did I look too long, did somebody notice me looking? I wish I could talk to a group of women and just tell them, because I know many don't really realize what a distraction it is. [Surely] they don't want the brethren to sin. I can't believe how some of these young girls dress. Don't they know the things we cherish, we must protect. I don't care about peer pressure; clothing is an opportunity to share your faith when people see a difference. Remember that man and (wo)man looks at the outward appearance. We have to be separated and yes a 'PECULIAR' people. Men are tempted and aroused by the things they SEE. David was tempted when he SAW Bathsheba; Herod was tempted when he SAW Salome dance; when Samson 'saw a women in Timnath,' he wanted her because her looks 'pleased' him."

"I want to mention the present trend of embossing brand names across the seat of women's trousers/pants/shorts/skirts. No imagination needed to explain that."

"I travel a bit, and as I'm walking through a crowded airport looking around, I tend more to notice things like short skirts, skirts or dresses with slits that come to or above the knee, low-cut blouses or dresses, sheer blouses, or tight-fitting anything. Clothing that accentuates or draws attention to one part of the body seems more noticeable to me. I believe that clothing absolutely can draw attention to the woman's body and that once attention is there, the potential, perhaps even likelihood, for lust isn't far behind."

"From what I see in the way many woman and teens dress, Christians included, many act like they are 'for sale' or are very ignorant of what they are doing to their image. That's the way I see things on this issue."

"The more skin I see, the more I have to force myself to look away from that individual. It brings back the past [before I was saved]. It seems like some women flaunt their bodies. What they are saying by their clothes, 'Don't look at my face, look at my body!' ... I am all for modesty and I wish all churches had a dress code. Not just in church but also out of church. Skin is a distraction! More skin; more sin."

"I agree with you about the lack of understanding from most women about the male weakness in the area of lust. The average Christian woman today seems to think, 'If you've got it, flaunt it.' I actually had one woman who used to be in my church saying that. ... God's final act of creation was His most beautiful. A normal man would agree with this. This sets us apart from the animal kingdom. In animals the male is the most attractive. The female is often rather dowdy. Humans are reversed. ... A godly woman can dress attractively and properly by following a few simple thoughts. Do the clothes she is wearing draw a man's eyes to her face or to her other body parts? Is the clothing she is wearing obviously feminine and modest and not made for men?"

"Thanks so much for addressing this issue. I am a Christian who has been doing street ministry for many years, and full time now for 20 years. I am also a single dad (wife died of cancer almost 9 years ago) of four sons, three under 18. I have concentrated on work in the public housing areas. To say I have seen it all would be an under statement. ONE OF THE SADDEST THINGS AND HARDEST TO FIGHT AGAINST HAS BEEN THE FACT THAT THE 'STREET' AND THE CHURCH NOW SEEM TO BE EQUAL IN THEIR APPROACH TO FEMALE SEXUALITY AND ITS EXPRESSION. THERE SEEMS TO BE NO BOTTOM TO THE LEVEL THAT MEMBERS OF THE CHURCH ARE WILLING TO ALLOW IN THE WAY OF WHAT CAN BE WORN TO CHURCH AND CHURCH FUNCTIONS. As a man who is deeply concerned that my sons do not get exposed to this type thing I find myself upset a lot about what goes on. It is obvious that many of these girls are not only NOT taught to be modest, but their parents have bought them the clothes that they wear to flaunt their sexuality in. Sadly enough, I would have to say that there is no part of the female body that I haven't seen in church. Short skirts, low cut blouses, halter tops, tiny two-piece bathing suits, and bathing suits with high cut in back seem to prevail in church activities. ... To go to the heart of the issue I would have to say that there appears to be many church men who revel in their daughters' budding sexuality."

"To answer your request on women's dress and modesty, I have to paraphrase a statement made many years ago by a Christian minister of national acclaim. His subject was Christian women and the way they dress that would tempt Christian men as well as worldly men to lust after them. It's been so many years ago that he preached the message that I can't quote directly, but in essence what he said was that any Christian man that said he wasn't affected by seeing a Christian sister in the short skirts, tight skirts etc. (in other words most of all of the items on your list, in fact I would include one or two more) the preacher would pay for that man's physical exam. Blunt but to the point. ... We as Christians are not to do anything to cause our Christian Brother or Sister to stumble, but THIS SUBJECT OF MODESTY (BOTH WOMEN AND MEN) IS NOT OFTEN PREACHED ON. ... I remember reading an article in a book about how culture has changed in the USA. In the early 1940's, a man could be reprimanded on the beach at Atlantic City for not wearing a top to his bathing suit. What we have now is close to nudity, especially for the women. My wife and I will not vacation at a beach so that we don't subject ourselves to the near nudity of the people there. ... One of the biggest mediums for temptation is the nudity that is seen on television (which we got rid of close to 30 years ago because of commercials and programming). Next to that are 99% of the magazine articles and advertising. But yet little if anything is mentioned from the pulpits about the influence of these two mediums."

"All of those items of female dress cause a real potential for lust. WHY SHOULD A MAN HAVE TO BATTLE WITH LUST DURING A CHURCH SERVICE WHEN IT IS HARD ENOUGH JUST TO WALK IN A WORLD FULL OF SENSUALITY? IF WOMEN ONLY KNEW THE SNARE OF TEMPTATION THAT IS SET BEFORE OUR EYES. Even if it is a fraction of a second and a man turns his head away, the battle can still rage in the mind just from a mere glimpse. I honestly believe that many of them know exactly what they are doing. Why else would they dress like the rebellious world?"

"It seems the last few years as the churches have grown more liberal and the women show more skin, I HAVE TO FIGHT HARDER TO KEEP MY MIND STRAIGHT. I am happily married. I do not and will not stray. … I wish women could just take the Bible for what it says. Yes, the Lord made us men this way. … I think the most beautiful thing God created on this earth is a woman, and Satan knows it, too. That is just the way I feel."

"As a Christian come back in from 20 years in the world, I can see this situation very well. I still tend to 'rate' (if you will) women physically by shape and presentation in my mind. This is a battle that must constantly be fought by one who gave in to lust in the past. A WOMAN IN A NICE DRESS WITH LITTLE EXPOSED IS PLEASING TO THE EYE AND STOPS AT THAT."

"I attend a very conservative independent fundamental Baptist church, where the pastor and his wife lead by example. Unfortunately, I see that oftentimes, some of the women in our church, though they always wear dresses or skirts to church and though they are always below the knee, THEY ARE STILL A BIT TOO CONCERNED WITH

'FASHION,' AND SOMETIMES COMPROMISE TRUE MODESTY FOR 'LOOKING GOOD' OR BEING FASHIONABLE. It is often an 'issue' for me. Many of these ladies are dear sweet Christian women, devoted wives, dedicated servants, and I don't believe they INTEND to be a distraction. I just don't think they realize!"

"My wife and I are the nursery directors at our church, and we are constantly having to interact with workers and mothers. Sometimes I find myself having to do a 'check' on where my eyes are being drawn, and where my thoughts are headed, and I have to PURPOSE to not think that way, or to just not look at them while I'm talking to them, to distract myself with something else (hmmm, that wall needs a new coat of paint, or that floor needs vacuuming, or we're out of paper towels). How do I tell them? I'm sure they would be mortified if they realized they were even remotely emitting a 'sexy' quality. That's not to say some women don't intend to look sexy. ... One woman in particular, who is very attractive (even my wife says so), USED to dress very stylish, in expensive, designer clothes that were hip, cool, young, modern, but seemed clueless as to the biblical boundaries she was overstepping. After our pastor preached on the subject of modesty, my wife and I noticed - IMMEDIATELY - that this lady's wardrobe changed completely. It was like the light went on and she responded with humility and gratitude for the message. Now, she still looks stylish, but is much more conservative, appropriate, and modest in her attire. It's truly a relief. Now when we see her coming, we're actually glad to see her because we know she's not going to make us feel uncomfortable because of her sexy-ish clothes."

"I would agree that while some women are out and out Jezebels there are others who do not understand how a man is affected by a woman's modesty (or lack thereof). One of my major concerns is that we have strayed from the question of how to standardize modesty. Almost anywhere I go anymore I hear the argument on the length of skirts. 'It's below the knee.' When did the definition of modesty begin with how far below the knee it goes? ... Why is it just length? Form-fitting, slit-skirted, bare legs, and everything else you mentioned in your list are a magnet for a man's eyes. While this has not been a problem at our church, it is becoming an issue with churches I would never have expected. I get irritated when I have to look in another direction rather than see an immodest woman in church. The point of the irritation is not that I am looking away but the fact that I have to do so in Independent Fundamental circles. ... I guess I get more and more frustrated with dress standards. We preach of the immorality of the world, television that is filled with homosexuality, nudity, and the internet filled with almost any type of perversion you want. OUR SOCIETY HAS DEGENERATED TO ANIMAL-LIKE SEXUALITY WHERE THERE ARE NO RULES AND LITTLE DISCUSSION OF CONSEQUENCES, AND OUR ANSWER SHOULD BE TO SHOW HOW DIFFERENT WE ARE FROM THEM (which is less and less). I do not care how different our ladies are from the world; this is not the standard of comparison. The standard of comparison is how much they are like Christ -- and He is nothing like this world. 'Ye therefore, beloved, seeing ye know [these things] before, beware lest ye also, being led away with the error of the wicked, fall from your own stedfastness' (2 Peter 3:17).

"Almost all of the styles you listed serve to in some way accentuate, reveal, or tantalize the senses of men. Men are very liable to visual temptation. Even Job realized that (Job 31:1). The Psalmist did, too (Psa. 101:3). The ladies need to know that there is a need to have a heart of modesty that will give them the desire to strengthen and honor their brothers in Christ. If that happens, modesty will be a matter of heart and dress, and not simply a legalistic issue."

"I suspect I have to deal with this most every day of my life. Consider the magazines in the grocery store checkout area. Most Christian women are oblivious to modesty, but the folks that design most of the clothes in most clothing stores where Christian women make purchases are not ignorant of what they are doing. The modestly dressed individual is a rare breed in this part of the country. I do know a few families, very few, who have decided to be different. But they cause me to look in amazement."

"I am a red blooded, fully functional, American man, who desires to have his thoughts and words be acceptable to God. I have been happily married for 28 years. THE BIBLICAL ISSUE OF MODESTY IS BEST UNDERSTOOD BY AN UNDERSTANDING OF DEFRAUDING. No one should take any action whereby he causes desires to be raised in another that cannot be righteously satisfied. ... That our society drenches every inch of media in sexually explicit advertising is a source of much temptation, sadness and concern for this man. Facing that sort of issue with Christian sisters in a church setting is most grievous. I believe the phrase 'long, loose and lots of it' should be the motto of Christian women's apparel. ... Before knowing her husband, my bride had no idea of how men think, or how easily stimulated they are. I hope my candor may be of some value to Christian sisters who are trying to live holy lives. I try to tell young ladies that I can influence for good, that the kind of fish you catch depends on what you bait your hook with, and where you cast your line. If you can't catch a man in church with a modest dress on, you don't want him anyway!"

"You are absolutely right about women not seeing these dangers. THEY CAN DEMAND BIBLE VERSES TO BACK UP THE ASSERTION THAT CERTAIN CLOTHES CAUSE LUST ALL DAY LONG, BUT THE TRUTH IS THAT IF THESE CLOTHES CAUSE MEN TO LUST, THEY ARE PARTICIPATING IN THE PROBLEM whether there are specific Scriptures to exclude every piece of clothing that designers can conceive."

"In my personal opinion, I think the styles that expose the bosom or the tight form of the bosom present the majority of the problem because it is more accepted to show that area in our society as opposed to the upper thigh or lower buttocks."

"Personally, I see women (including independent Baptist church-goers and staff) causing potential for lust in all the clothing you listed. The point is that it is not the type of clothing that can trip a man up; rather it is the amount and the level of cling to the body. ... when I see women dressing as I described above, I can't avoid wondering why they are 'advertising' their flesh. Is it because they are lacking in Christian character?"

"My wife was taught as a little girl that all attention should be drawn to her face, and that rule has been a great guideline."

"It's not always what the attire is but how it is worn and the woman herself. ... Excessive use of perfume and make up -- both designed to draw men; they should be used with wisdom. Also, flirtatious natures and wanting to be noticed by the opposite sex should be reigned in."

"It is the duty of every husband to make sure his wife is properly dressed, not only for Church but all the time. ... I have been blessed with a modest wife. Men are weak in the area of sex and need 'the handbrake' of a modest woman to keep him on track and his thoughts in line."

"I am certainly not proud to have to say that all of the above items of clothing on women cause a real potential for lust, but for me it is the case. OF ALL OF MY CLOSE BROTHERS IN THE LORD WHOM I HAVE TALKED WITH ON THIS SUBJECT OVER TIME, ALL ARE IN AGREEMENT THAT THEY STRUGGLE WITH LUST; and it is so few women, at least where I am, that dress modestly or even have a single clue that there is a Biblical instruction for them to do so. I am so thankful for my Pastor's wife (they are new here and have planted a new Church in my city) and her decision to dress modestly."

"Maybe I just have a problem with lust, but I know my own heart. There is no godly, good reason that I should ever see from 'the neck to the knees' of any woman other than my wife."

"IT IS AMAZING TO ME THAT HUSBANDS, FATHERS, ETC., WOULD ALLOW THEIR WOMEN OUT IN PUBLIC WEARING SOME OF THE THINGS WOMEN WEAR. Have they no idea the thoughts of other men? Shame on them."

"There is a term 'not leaving anything to the imagination.' Our Father knows, as does any man, that men do not need any encouragement at all, let alone a less than reverent dress style. The fleshly man is full of imagination. … I cannot think of even one of the styles listed that are appropriate for women. Unfortunately, I see them in churches and 'Christian Schools' every day."

"Blessings to you for writing on this subject. There is nothing I detest more than women dressed immodestly anywhere, but most especially in church. This is one more way for Satan to take men's minds off of the worship of their Heavenly Father! Women should not wear anything which exposes or draws a man's attention to [those] areas [that are] conducive to male lust. OH HOW I WISH MODEST DRESSING WOULD COME BACK INTO STYLE -- THAT BOTH MEN AND WOMEN WOULD HAVE MORE SELF RESPECT IN GENERAL, AND PARTICULARLY MORE RESPECT OF THE LORD'S HOUSE."

"Whatever standard the parent lives before and requires of his/her children, the easier it will be for the child to maintain that standard. Usually the child never has higher standards than the parent. If we expect lawyers, ambassadors, etc. to look respectful and above the normal standard, shouldn't Christians do the same?"

"Another apparel item that may be worth mentioning is knee-high leather boots. These seem to be more and more prevalent among Christian women. In my opinion, these boots scream sensuality and area real potential for generating lust. I may be completely off base on this as my view is certainly tainted from years of pornography, womanizing, immorality, spending a lot of time at bars...etc. (from my teen years until my mid twenties when I was saved). During those days, however, when a woman wore knee high boots, it would certainly attract attention for all of the wrong reasons. Perhaps Christian women are not aware of this? Overall, on the issue of modesty, I COMPLETELY AGREE THAT MANY WOMEN DO NOT UNDERSTAND HOW MEN LOOK AT THINGS IN THIS REALM. I SUSPECT FOR MANY MEN, INCLUDING ME, THAT LUST IS A DAILY BATTLE. I DESIRE FOR MY CHURCH FAMILY AND CHRISTIAN FRIENDS TO BE A SAFE HAVEN FROM TEMPTATION."

"If such things draw the attention of normal, godly, Christian men, by definition they are immodest, no matter what the women think."

"It is my conviction that all of the female dress items listed are immodest for women. I am 68 years old and have been married to a wonderful, modest lady for 49 years. I am appalled at how so many women dress even in church. My mother is 88 years old and worked in the cotton fields alongside my father back when we did it all by hand. I've never seen my mother or either of my grandmothers in pants or shorts and they all worked in the fields. I have never seen any of the women who raised me in any of the items that you mentioned. I thank God for the example they were to me. By the way, they all washed their clothes by hand and I never saw any women's undergarments hanging out on the clothes line for all that passed by to look at. Proving that their modesty went far deeper than what they put on their bodies. It was in their heart."

"When my wife and I were first married, she wore pants. I didn't tell her to stop, although she would have if I told her to. She would have quit wearing pants but she would have resented me for telling her to do so. She had to quit wearing them because she was convicted by the Holy Spirit and God's Word. She was convicted and she quit wearing pants. In fact, she dresses so modestly that people stare at her because she dresses differently and not because she's showing something off. I am proud of her stance as a Christian because she dresses this way in obedience to the Word of God and not only in obedience to me."

"I don't know how women can 'not' know the impact their dress has on men. In fact I believe they do (more than they say or let on). One thing I see in my church is tight clothing. Oh, it may very well be covering but it is revealing the shape in a woman. This can be even more tantalizing to a man. I once was at a conference and the preacher asked a very strong Christian couple (wife modestly dressed) who do you dress for (question to the wife) and she said her husband. The preacher and the congregation gave their amens. I thought about that answer and it was an answer I would have wanted my wife to give until to a few years before. Now she knows I would want her to dress for the Lord Jesus Christ Himself. I have the potential to be carnal, and in the flesh and to want to see her in less modest apparel. That would never be the case with our Lord. Thus I told her to dress for Jesus Christ."

"Our church teaches and preaches separation. Our pastor has even compiled a small booklet on modest dress. Having said all that, we have had and still do have problems. In order to be a choir member or teach Sunday School, etc., we must sign a form saying we agree to the dress standards as well as many other standards of conduct. What I have seen is, yes, they are wearing dresses, but many are far from modest. I have had my wife ask me, 'Did you see what so and so was wearing?' I am honest with her and I tell her of course I did! I am a man and when a lady exposes 50% of her breasts I can't help but notice. I told her I don't ogle but it is a part of a woman that men find attractive, so there I am in God's house trying to worship God and hear from His Word and I see these things. But she is wearing a dress!! Form fitting clothing is another area that is a problem. A lady can be actually wearing a reasonably nice dress that meets the standard, at least in their mind it does, but the problem is that it is at least a size too small for her! These folks are rarely confronted because they are wearing a dress, you know! I believe we easily forget modesty and become lost in 'I'm wearing a dress attitude.' To be honest I have seen more modest pants on many lost ladies than the 'dresses on our standard-signing church ladies.' I'm not for pants; I'm just referring to our hypocrisy! It shows either a lack of discernment on their part or a worldly desire to show off their body, maybe both. ... Sorry to vent but this has hit close to home as I have tried to protect teenagers from what they see 'in church.' I BELIEVE THERE IS A TREMENDOUS LACK OF UNDERSTANDING ON THE PART OF MOST WOMEN ABOUT WHAT THEY WEAR AND WHY. ... As I said, our church teaches and preaches on these things and they do a good job teaching it. It is a spiritual issue. They know the facts. It is accepting them and living by them that is the problem. I have heard, 'They just want us to look like old women.' If that means to dress modestly, then, yes, please try to look at the older women who are trying to teach the younger, as Titus says, through example."

"As I was not saved until I was an adult, I was like most men; I enjoyed the sight of the female form. Without Christ, I had no reason not to indulge my lusts when I looked at immodestly dressed women. There is no shortage of flesh in our culture; the movies, TV, music videos, internet, etc., all promote it. After I was saved, God began to show me through his word to flee youthful lusts and to be like Job who made a covenant with his eyes not to look upon a maid. You listed several types of clothing and asked which ones were areas of temptation. My answer would be 'all of them!' As my wife and I began to grow in the Lord, I made the comment to her that IF THE AVERAGE WOMAN KNEW HOW THE

AVERAGE MAN THINKS IT WOULD CAUSE HER TO DRESS A LOT DIFFERENTLY. I don't think women realize just how much they expose themselves by the style of the clothes they wear (or don't wear, as the case may be)."

"The stark difference between Biblical modesty and femininity was illustrated one night as another preacher and I, along with our wives and families, were on the street in a large city near our home preaching and passing out gospel tracts during a music festival. Two young women, who were dressed very provocatively, walked by and received the cat-calls and lewd remarks of a couple of young guys. The boys then turned and saw my wife standing there (she is 32), dressed in a modest skirt and top and said, 'Oh, sorry ma'am!' Ladies need to understand, that how they are dressed says a lot about who they are, and determines to some extent how they will be treated. Scripture backs this up (Proverbs 7, Genesis 38:15-16)."

"PASTORS NEED TO DEAL WITH THIS ISSUE AS MORE THAN JUST A 'WHEN YOU COME TO CHURCH' THING. I believe we have created a double standard in our independent Baptist churches in that the only time dress is dealt with is when people are taught that they ought to come to church 'dressed right,' but not many deal with the fact that believers are to glorify God in all things, everyday, including how we dress. Christian women have a responsibility before the Lord to be obedient to the Bible's admonitions concerning dress. They also have a responsibility to their brothers in the Lord, not to cast a stumbling block before them in the way that they dress."

"I am 60 years old and even as a younger, unsaved man, it always seemed strange to see church-going women dressed in that manner (and I understand many felt they needed to do so to attract a man) and now, in many of the more liberal churches, and some so-called fundamental ones, the manner of dress seems to be according to one's own preference and not based on the Bible's teaching of decent dress. I'm also still amazed that some church-going men like their wives to dress in that way."

"I became a born again believer in Jesus Christ when I was 34. Our family left the Methodist church and switched to a large popular Southern Baptist Church. We eventually left the Southern Baptist Church, and one of the biggest reasons is because women dressed so immodestly, I felt I was in a lingerie show. I would have to walk the halls of the church with my head hung to avoid the display of flesh. ... We became quickly disappointed that the church often undermined our own family's standards. ... Two years ago, our family finally switched to a Fundamental Independent Bible believing Baptist church and we really love serving the Lord and being with believers of like precious faith and with standards. ... I believe if godly women understood the effect they can have on a godly man they would dress differently. I have daughters and I constantly have to instruct them on what men think of immodestly dressed women and correct their dress."

"Thank you for addressing this serious problem. I agree that most Christian women do not seem to understand how that the way they dress affects men. Unfortunately, some do understand and they enjoy dressing in a way that attracts the attention of men. ... We are living in the last part of the last days. Demon influence and demon possession is rampant. Evil triumphs when the church does nothing. ONE SIGN OF DEMON ACTIVITY IS NUDITY AND LEWD DRESS. MEN RESPOND BY SIGHT. Sight arouses their sexual drive. Anything that exposes highlights or outlines the torso and thigh is lustful dress. The Word of God is clear that a man who lusts after a woman is guilty of adultery along with her. I told my people last Sunday that if the women dress inappropriately and go to town, causing four men to look and lust, they will be held accountable for participating in committing adultery."

"As a man, a Christian, and a pastor, I believe modesty is perhaps the most important issue in dress, whether among the church or otherwise, because, I'M TELLING YOU, MEN NOTICE, MEN LOOK, AND MEN LUST, EVEN THE GOOD ONES. I know many women say, 'Well, that's their problem, not mine!' But while we men will answer for our lust, the ladies will answer for doing something that causes another to fall into sin. Ladies, understand, your dress DOES effect us, and as such, you should prayerful consider what you wear. Men are created in such a way as to be stimulated by sight--so when we see a lady, pretty, or sometimes not, we are stimulated by the sight of their flesh. It's just the way we are."

"Ladies, please, dress with modesty. DRESS AS YOU WOULD IF JESUS WERE SITTING NEXT TO YOU. And He is, by the way, both because the Christian is indwelt by the Holy Spirit and because He has promised to be there when two or three are gathered together in His name. Jesus is sitting next to you!"

"I am a member of a fundamental church and am sad to say that many of these worldly ways are finding their way into our church. MAY GOD SEND HIS HOLY SPIRIT TO MOVE IN OUR MIDST SO THAT A REVIVAL WOULD BREAK FORTH."

Bibliography

Allison, Mike. *Legalism: A Smokescreen*. Murfreesboro, TN: Sword of the Lord, 1986. 15 p.

———. *Preaching Standards Right or Wrong?* Shelbyville, TN: Bible and Literature Missionary Foundation, 1984. 71 p.

Cooper, Wendy. *Hair*. New York: Stein and Day, 1971. 240 p.

Corle, Cathy. *What in the World Should I Wear?* Claysburg, PA: Revival Fires, 1992. 44 p.

Feldhahn, Shaunti. *For Women Only: What You Need to Know about the Inner Lives of Men*. Sisters, OR: Multnomah Publishers, 2004. 188 p.

Galyean, Eddie R. *Biblical Modesty*. Ft. Pierce, FL: Eddie Galyean, 1993. 106 p.

Handford, Elizabeth Rice. *Your Clothes Say It For You*. Murfreesboro, TN: Sword of the Lord, 1976. 101 p.

Jones, Milton. *The Believer's Relationship to the World*. Lizella, GA: Fountain of Life Ministries, nd. 28 p.

Kidd, David. *The Fall and Rise of Christian Standards: Thinking Biblically about Dress and Appearance*. Zulon Press, 2005. 206 p.

Lackey, Bruce. *Bible Guidelines for Clothing*. Port Huron, MI: Way of Life Literature, nd. 20 p.

Martin, Curtis. *God's Standard for Dress*. Ft. Morgan, CO: Martin Publishing, 1995. 15 p.

Rice, John R. *Bobbed Hair, Bossy Wives, and Women Preachers*. Murfreesboro, TN: Sword of the Lord, 1941. 91 p.

Rubinstein, Ruth P. *Dress Codes: Meanings and Messages in American Culture*. Boulder, CO: Westview Press, 1995. 314 p.

Schrock, Simon. *What Shall the Redeemed Wear?* Harrisonburg, VA: printed by Campbell Copy Center, 2000. 120 p.

Starr, Shirley M., and Lori L. Waltemyer. *Dress: The Heart of the Matter*. Kearney, NE: Morris Publishing, 2003. 78 p.

Tassell, Paul, and Robert Regal. *Carelessness and Casualness in Worship: in Dress and in Singing*. Middletown, CT: The Middletown Bible Church, nd. 12 p.